T0334170

Cambridge Elements

Elements in Women Theatre Makers
edited by
Elaine Aston
Lancaster University
Melissa Sihra
Trinity College Dublin

#WAKINGTHEFEMINISTS AND THE DATA-DRIVEN REVOLUTION IN IRISH THEATRE

Claire Keogh
Independent Scholar

CAMBRIDGE
UNIVERSITY PRESS

Shaftesbury Road, Cambridge CB2 8EA, United Kingdom

One Liberty Plaza, 20th Floor, New York, NY 10006, USA

477 Williamstown Road, Port Melbourne, VIC 3207, Australia

314–321, 3rd Floor, Plot 3, Splendor Forum, Jasola District Centre, New Delhi – 110025, India

103 Penang Road, #05–06/07, Visioncrest Commercial, Singapore 238467

Cambridge University Press is part of Cambridge University Press & Assessment, a department of the University of Cambridge.

We share the University's mission to contribute to society through the pursuit of education, learning and research at the highest international levels of excellence.

www.cambridge.org
Information on this title: www.cambridge.org/9781009523103

DOI: 10.1017/9781009523066

© Claire Keogh 2025

When citing this work, please include a reference to the DOI 10.1017/9781009523066

First published 2025

A catalogue record for this publication is available from the British Library

ISBN 978-1-009-52310-3 Hardback
ISBN 978-1-009-52309-7 Paperback
ISSN 2634-2391 (online)
ISSN 2634-2383 (print)

#WakingTheFeminists and the Data-Driven Revolution in Irish Theatre

Elements in Women Theatre Makers

DOI: 10.1017/9781009523066
First published online: January 2025

Claire Keogh
Independent Scholar
Author for correspondence: Claire Keogh, ckeogh4@tcd.ie

Abstract: #WakingTheFeminists was a year-long grassroots campaign for gender equality in Irish theatre. Prompted by the gender disparity of Ireland's Abbey Theatre's 2016 programme, 'Waking the Nation', Lian Bell posted a Facebook message that sparked a surge of feminist fury that ignited the #WakingTheFeminists movement. This Element considers the movement both as digital feminist activism and as part of the growing trend of data feminism, by analysing how its combined use of connective and collective action, and qualitative and quantitative data, was critical to its success. It contextualises the movement historically in relation to a series of feminist controversies in Irish theatre since 1990, before considering its impact on both policy and cultural changes across the Irish arts sector. #WakingTheFeminists' national and international resonance derived from its research-informed strategy which made it the most effective campaign for gender equality in the history of Irish theatre.

Keywords: #WakingTheFeminists, Abbey Theatre, gender counts, gender equality, networked feminism

ISBNs: 9781009523103 (HB), 9781009523097 (PB), 9781009523066 (OC)
ISSNs: 2634-2391 (online), 2634-2383 (print)

Contents

Introduction: A Feminist Revolution in Irish Theatre

#WakingTheFeminists caused a seismic shift in Irish theatre in 2015 when a grassroots feminist movement held the industry's top players to account for sexism, unconscious bias, and gender inequality. The movement began with a Facebook post published by Arts Manager and Designer, Lian Bell, in an exasperated response to the announcement of the Abbey Theatre's 2016 programme, 'Waking the Nation', which included ten plays, only one of which was written by a woman and just three were to be directed by women. In disbelief at the blatant disparity, Bell wrote: 'Happy to be proven wrong, if I've missed something major in my flurry of righteous indignation. But, like, REALLY?' (Bell, 2015). Bell's Facebook comment initiated an explosive conversation about the treatment of women in Irish theatre that rapidly spread to Twitter, the mainstream media, and beyond. The initial anger and outrage expressed online grew into a coordinated movement designed to hold the Irish theatre industry to account for its persistent and gross gender inequality. #WakingTheFeminists' year-long campaign centred on three live events, the first of which was held at the Abbey Theatre on 12 November 2015 and was the fastest selling event in the theatre's history. Counting, an important aspect of Bell's original post, became a key part of the campaign, which culminated in the publication of a report that examined productions by the top ten funded Irish theatre organisations between 2006 and 2015, and found 'that Irish theatre has a significant gender problem' (Donohue et al., 2017: 7). With origins on social media, #WakingTheFeminists could have been another flash of online outrage, but what unfolded in late 2015 and throughout 2016 was a strategic campaign for gender equality that has had an impressive impact on Irish culture.

The Abbey Theatre's 'Waking the Nation' programme was intended to mark one hundred years since the armed insurrection against British rule, known as the Easter Rising.[1] The programme was designed to 'interrogate and question the legacy of the Easter Rising rather than celebrate the centenary' (Blake Knox, 2015a). 'Waking the Nation' included four 'Masterpieces' to be presented on the main stage: *The Plough and the Stars* by Sean O'Casey, *Othello* by William Shakespeare, *The Wake* by Tom Murphy, and *Observe the Sons of Ulster Marching Towards the Somme* by Frank McGuinness (see

---

[1] The Easter Rising occurred when a group of rebels took over the General Post Office in Dublin on Easter Monday, 1916, and read the 'Proclamation of the Irish Republic', which asserted the sovereignty and independence of Ireland. The rebels fought for a week against heavy British artillery before surrendering. Although the rebellion failed, the execution of sixteen of its leaders sparked a new wave of public support for Irish freedom. The Irish War of Independence (1919–21) that followed resulted in the partition of Ireland into two territories, the independent Irish Free State (now Republic of Ireland) and British-controlled Northern Ireland, prompting civil war in 1922.

Figure 1). These were supported by four 'New Irish Plays' in the smaller Peacock space: *Of This Brave Time* by Jimmy Murphy, *Cyprus Avenue* by David Ireland, *Tina's Idea of Fun* by Sean P. Summers, and *Town is Dead* by Phillip McMahon with music by Raymond Scannell (see Figure 2). The 'Dialogue & Debate' portion of the programme included The Theatre of Change Symposium and a short run of the Palestinian play, *New Middle East* by Mutaz Abu Saleh, also in the Peacock. The 'Schools & Community' programme included the only play by a woman, *Me, Mollser* by Ali White, alongside the All Island Schools Drama Competition (see Figure 3). Designed as a companion piece to Sean O'Casey's *The Plough and the Stars*, *Me Mollser* had already been touring since 2012 as part of the Abbey Theatre's Community and Education programme and would not appear on the stages of the national theatre in 2016. This meant that 'the commemorative season would not present any writing by women in the theatre building itself' (Quigley, 2018: 85). Women were similarly under-represented as directors in the programme. Of the ten productions, three were directed by women: Vicky Featherstone directed *Cyprus Avenue*, Annabelle Comyn worked on *The Wake*, and Sarah Fitzgibbon was the director of *Me, Mollser*. Despite drawing heavily on the fact that an Abbey Theatre actress, Helena Moloney, had fought in 1916 throughout the programme's marketing, the small representation of women in generative creative roles in the programme prompted uproar.

Bell's Facebook post (Figure 4) tapped into a well of latent frustration about the way women were being excluded, ignored, and undermined within Irish theatre. However, the remarkable events that followed solidified what might have been a fizzle of feminist frustration into a slick campaign for change. At 4 PM, on Thursday, 29 October 2015, as outrage continued to grow on Facebook, the Abbey Theatre's Director, Fiach Mac Conghail, hosted an impromptu question-and-answer session on Twitter, as he travelled to the airport for a holiday. In a series of tweets (Twitter posts), interrupted by blackouts as his coach travelled through the Dublin Port Tunnel, Mac Conghail defended his programme with vim:

> I'm sorry that I have no female playwrights next season. But I'm not going to produce a play that is not ready and undermine the writer #wtn

> I don't and haven't programmed plays or productions on a gender basis. I took decisions based on who I admired and wanted to work with.

> All my new play choices are based on the quality of the play, form and theme. It's my call and I'm pleased with the plays I picked for #wtn

> In programming any season I want to make sure that the plays are good (imho), ready and delivered. 1/2

Masterpieces

'We need new myths that not only carry the burden of history but fly from it, making something new.'

President Michael D. Higgins
*Speaking at the Theatre of Literary Symposium,
16 January 2014*

THE PLOUGH AND THE STARS

BY Sean O'Casey | DIRECTOR Sean Holmes

This provocative play is essential to our understanding of the legacy of the 1916 Rising. Olivier Award-winning director Sean Holmes will bring a new and challenging perspective to Sean O'Casey's masterpiece.

Featuring Ian-Lloyd Anderson as Jack and Kate Stanley Brennan as Nora.

...

9 March – 23 April | on the Abbey stage

THE PLOUGH AND THE STARS *On Tour*

Following performances at the Abbey Theatre, *The Plough and the Stars* will embark on a tour of Ireland and North America.

IRISH TOUR
Cork Opera House
The National Opera House, Wexford
Lime Tree Theatre, Limerick
Town Hall Theatre, Galway

NORTH AMERICAN TOUR
In association with Cusack Projects Limited
IRELAND 100: Celebrating a Century of
Irish Arts and Culture at the Kennedy Center
in Washington, DC
American Repertory Theater, Harvard University,
Massachusetts
Annenberg Center for the Performing Arts,
University of Pennsylvania
Peak Performances at Montclair State University,
New Jersey
Southern Theatre, Columbus, Ohio presented by
CAPA and The Ohio State University

OTHELLO

BY William Shakespeare | DIRECTOR Joe Dowling

In 2016, on the 400th anniversary of Shakespeare's death we are proud to present this extraordinary state of the nation play, featuring Peter Macon as Othello and Marty Rea as Iago.

...

5 May – 11 June | on the Abbey stage

THE WAKE

BY Tom Murphy | DIRECTOR Annabelle Comyn

Our long-awaited revival of *The Wake* is an excoriating critique of the materialism of Irish life. It's a wake for our dream of a state with the family at its heart.

...

22 June – 30 July | on the Abbey stage

OBSERVE THE SONS OF ULSTER MARCHING TOWARDS THE SOMME *On Tour*

Observe the Sons of Ulster Marching Towards the Somme will be on an extensive tour of Britain and Northern Ireland before arriving in Dublin.

BRITISH TOUR
Citizens Theatre
Liverpool Playhouse

A co-production with RealLiong,
Citizens Theatre, Liverpool Everyman
& Playhouse Theatre

OBSERVE THE SONS OF ULSTER MARCHING TOWARDS THE SOMME

BY Frank McGuinness DIRECTOR Jeremy Herrin

On 1 July 1916, the 36th (Ulster) Division took part in one of the bloodiest battles in human history. The Battle of the Somme. One hundred years on, the Abbey Theatre presents a major new co-production of this iconic war play by Frank McGuinness.

...

6 August – 24 September | on the Abbey stage

NORTHERN IRISH TOUR
Tour dates in Northern Ireland are co-presented with the Lyric Theatre, Belfast. The tour will open on the Danske Bank stage at the Lyric Theatre, before travelling to venues throughout Northern Ireland.

Figure 1 The 'Masterpieces' section of the Abbey Theatre's 'Waking the Nation' leaflet. Courtesy of the Abbey Theatre Archive.

Figure 2 The 'New Irish Plays' section of the Abbey Theatre's 'Waking the
Nation' leaflet. Courtesy of the Abbey Theatre Archive.

> I'm not going to expose any playwright, man or woman, by producing a play
> that's not ready. Always a challenge in programming 2/2

> Also, sometimes the plays and ideas that we have commissioned by and about
> women just don't work out. That has happened. Them the breaks.[2]

His comment, 'Them the breaks', was incendiary to the growing protest (see
Figure 5). Belinda McKeon, who was under commission at the Abbey at the
time, was among his most prominent interrogators on Twitter. However, Mac
Conghail's responses to her questions about his programme with personal
comments on her commission, like 'I'm still waiting for your next draft' and
'Write your play', did not help his position (Burns, 2015). Nor did the treatment
of the only woman writer in 'Waking the Nation', Ali White, who had not been

---

[2] *#wtn* stands for 'Waking the Nation'; *imho* is an acronym for 'in my humble opinion'. Following
significant backlash, Mac Conghail later deleted some of these tweets, including the seditious
'Them the breaks'. He has since deleted his Twitter account (@fmacconghail).

Figure 3 The 'Dialogue & Debate' and 'Schools & Community' sections of the Abbey Theatre's 'Waking the Nation' leaflet, featuring *Me, Mollser* by Ali White. Courtesy of the Abbey Theatre Archive.

invited to the programme launch and whose existence was effectively erased by these tweets. White wrote on Facebook, 'Fiach tweets that he's sorry he hasn't any female playwrights in the next season. So . . . . . I'm not a playwright then? And my play has become "a specially commissioned monologue for children." So . . . . . it's not a play?'[3] Rather than quell the rising discontent, Mac Conghail's comments added fuel to the fire, and the limbo caused by his temporary absence from the country created space in which the dissenters could mobilise.

Following Mac Conghail's reckless Twitter storm, testimonies from many artists published online revealed the extent of the anger and frustration felt by women working in the industry. Within days, calls began to be made for a public meeting,

---

[3] www.wakingthefeminists.org/ali-white/.

Just did a quick tot up of the Abbey Theatre's 2016 programme 'Waking the Nation' launched moments ago.
Of the 10 listed productions on the website there are:
9 male and 1 female writers (of Me, Mollser - which is already touring in 2015) and 7 male and 2 female directors (again, one is of Me, Mollser).
I can't see a credit for who's directing The Wake, so that might redress the balance a little. Though it did take me a good bit of searching to come up with a director's name for Me, Mollser as Sarah Fitzgibbon doesn't seem to be credited on the Abbey's website.
Adding to that the main stage show that's on through January 2016, and Pan Pan's revival of the (wonderful) All That Fall in February, there's another two men directing plays by a further two men.
Happy to be proven wrong, if I've missed something major in my flurry of righteous indignation.
But, like, REALLY?

👍 67 👎 10

Figure 4 Lian Bell's first Facebook post in response to the announcement of the Abbey Theatre's 'Waking the Nation' programme on 28 October 2015. #WakingTheFeminists collection, courtesy of the National Library of Ireland.

Fiach Mac Conghail @fmacconghail · Oct 29
Also, sometimes plays and ideas that we have commissioned by and about women just don't work out. That has happened. Them the breaks.

⤺   ⇄ 3   ★ 1   • • •

Figure 5 Tweet sent by Abbey Theatre Director, Fiach Mac Conghail (@fmacconghail), on 29 October 2015 containing the phrase 'Them the Breaks'.

and on Saturday, 31 October, Lian Bell began to share images of some of the conversations that had been happening on private Facebook pages to her public Twitter account. Permission had been sought from each individual mentioned in the conversations before they were shared and the posts on Twitter were all tagged with the #WakingTheFeminists hashtag, coined a day previously by director, Maeve Stone (see Figure 6). By Wednesday, 4 November, the hashtag, #WakingTheFeminists, was trending on Twitter as a stream of messages of support from theatre organisations bolstered the movement's profile. The next day, just eight days after the 'Waking the Nation' announcement, fourteen theatre workers met at the offices of Rough Magic Theatre Company to plan the first live event. Those in

Figure 6 Tweet featuring first use of the phrase, 'Waking the Feminists', sent by Maeve Stone (@maevestone) on 30 October 2015.

attendance were Lian Bell, Siobhán Bourke and Jane Daly (Irish Theatre Institute), Anne Clarke (Landmark Productions), Loughlin Deegan (The Lir Academy), Sarah Durcan (Science Gallery International, ex. Dublin Fringe Festival, Dublin Theatre Festival & Corn Exchange), Kate Ferris (The Lir Academy and WillFredd), Maria Fleming (The Ark), Gavin Kostick (Fishamble: The New Play Company), Jo Mangan (The Performance Corporation), Tríona Ní Dhuibhir (Dublin Theatre Festival), Dairne O'Sullivan (freelance PR), Lynne Parker (Rough Magic), and Caroline Williams (Rough Magic, ex. Glasshouse Productions). These were joined at subsequent meetings by Róise Goan (freelance), Irma McLoughlin (Theatre Forum), Cian O'Brien (Project Arts Centre), among many others.[4] The vast producing and organisational experience among this group meant that the campaign evolved with exceptional attention to detail and speed.

When Mac Conghail returned from his holiday on Friday, 6 November, he issued a letter of apology, stating that he regretted the gender imbalance in 'Waking the Nation'. He wrote, 'The fact that I haven't programmed a new play by a female playwright is not something I can defend' and that the experience had presented 'a professional challenge' that made him 'question the filters and factors that influence [his] decision-making'.[5] This was followed on Monday, 9 November, by a statement from the Board and Director of the Abbey Theatre acknowledging that 'the 2016 programme does not represent gender equality'.[6] However, these apologies were already too late, and in the interim, a team of highly motivated activists had formed and planned a major live event, thus laying the foundations for what would become a year-long campaign for gender equality that would not only penetrate the core of

---

[4] www.wakingthefeminists.org/about-wtf/timeline/.

[5] https://web.archive.org/web/20160319035756/http://www.abbeytheatre.ie/an-open-letter-on-debate-on-wakingthenation-wakingthefeminists.

[6] https://web.archive.org/web/20160321055616/http://www.abbeytheatre.ie/statement-on-behalf-of-the-board-and-director-of-the-abbey-theatre/.

the Irish theatre sector but have widespread reach throughout the arts sector in Ireland and internationally.

By the time this statement from the Abbey Theatre was published, the #WakingTheFeminists juggernaut was already in full force. Within eight days of the first #WakingTheFeminists tweet, the campaign already had a mission statement, a website, created by director, Oonagh Murphy, in collaboration with digital marketer and dramaturg, Noelia Ruiz, official Twitter, Instagram, and Gmail accounts, and the Abbey Theatre secured as the venue for the first event. The #WakingTheFeminists hashtag, which had been adopted across social media, became the official name of the movement, embraced partly because of its abbreviation to the acronym #WTF. Playing on the fact that 'Waking the Nation' was designed to mark the centenary of the Easter Rising, Eleanor Methven also coined an alternative name, The Estrogen Rising. Playwright and designer, Kate Heffernan, launched the campaign's brand with a series of badge designs for the public event. The huge banner that formed the centrepiece of the photograph taken outside the Abbey Theatre before that first event was created by another designer, Molly O'Cathain, who was a student at the time (see Figure 7).[7] O'Cathain's description of the request for help she received

Figure 7 Group photo taken outside the Abbey Theatre before the first #WakingTheFeminists public meeting on 12 November 2015, featuring the banner created by Molly O'Cathain. Photographer: Fiona Morgan.

---

[7] www.wakingthefeminists.org/about-wtf/timeline/.

from Sarah Durcan as being like 'a call to arms; a "your country needs you" moment' captures a sense of the urgency and importance with which each individual contribution to the event was considered (Bell, 2021).

Amid the initial flurry of activity on social media, #WakingTheFeminists received public backing, not only in Ireland but from the arts community internationally with celebrities including Meryl Streep and Debra Messing giving their support to the cause. This support helped to push the excitement about the public event to fever-pitch and when tickets for the meeting were released, they were snapped up in seven minutes. The Abbey Theatre auditorium was packed to capacity for that first public meeting, which began at 1 PM on Thursday, 12 November. While thirty women spoke from the Abbey stage of their personal experiences of gender-based discrimination at the national theatre and beyond, many more gathered in the foyer and bar to listen to the event via a live feed. A further 1,800 people watched a live stream via the video streaming application, Periscope. The atmosphere was angry, impassioned, and electric. Speeches from the stage were followed by many more voices from the floor, including Fiach Mac Conghail's, who, laudably, said that he was listening. The afternoon concluded with the entire auditorium on their feet dancing to Aretha Franklin's 'Respect'. The rousing, cathartic release of the music also revealed the intent of the room: these women were not requesting, but demanding, to be treated equally. Over ten thousand tweets[8] using the hashtag #WakingTheFeminists were sent throughout the day and a week later, a petition calling for equality with over 5,596 signatures was delivered to the Abbey Theatre.

The campaign's rapid-fire start was bolstered by the significant support it was receiving both within the theatre community and in the mainstream media. However, there were voices of dissent. Jimmy Murphy, one of the playwrights featured in 'Waking the Nation', wrote a letter to *The Irish Times*, saying, 'The Abbey Theatre is under no obligation to foist poorly written plays on a paying audience just to fulfil a programme and address balance. Anyone who thinks otherwise is deluded' (Murphy, 2015). John Delaney responded the next day with the rebuke that 'anyone who thinks the Abbey has not already foisted hundreds of poorly written plays by men upon its beleaguered audience is clearly deluded' (Delaney, 2015). Kevin Myers rolled out the well-rehearsed arguments that women are hysterical in a grandiloquent description of the social media storm as 'a week of Fallopia Whynge doing her online worst with foam, froth, fang and claw' (Myers, 2015). His argument centred on the question of why women have failed to achieve the same status writing plays as they have writing novels. Rhetorically, he asked, 'Is it because misogynistic theatreowners loathe profit, preferring instead to stage

---

[8] https://twitter.com/tanyadean/status/664877608237158400.

wretched, lossmaking plays by incompetent men rather than mount superior and wealth-generating plays by women?' (Myers, 2015). This question has, in fact, been answered affirmatively by Emily Glassberg Sands, who found that for the period between 1999 and 2009, 'while less than one-eighth of productions on Broadway are female-written, female-written plays on supposedly profit-maximizing Broadway over the past decade averaged significantly higher revenues than did their male-written counterparts' (Glassberg Sands, 2009: 105). The criticisms by Murphy and Myers had already been anticipated and addressed in an article by Una Mullally, who wrote that when men 'say things such as "do you expect plays to be programmed just because they're by women?" these statements are designed to shut down the conversation and assert male ownership over art' (Mullally, 2015). With prescience, she continued, 'Funnily enough, you'll find that it's those who benefit from the status quo who seek to maintain it' (Mullally, 2015). These isolated voices of dissent were convincingly and comprehensively outnumbered by supporters of the campaign, across the arts, the media, and the general public. In fact, the overwhelming reaction to #WakingTheFeminists was embarrassment by a theatre community that had prided itself on its liberal values. As Sarah Durcan said at #WakingTheFeminists' second public event, 'It's unsettling for each of us to realise that we are not quite the liberal, inclusive, meritocracy we believed our sector to be' (#WakingTheFeminists, 2016b).

The visibility of the campaign was significantly bolstered by the messages of support that came from across the Irish arts sector, and from theatre and film communities globally. Feminist groups like Guerrilla Girls, Clean Break Theatre Company in the UK, the Women's Project Theater in New York, and Women in Theatre and Screen, Australia all tweeted messages of support. Celebrities including Christine Baranski, Saoirse Ronan, Simon Callow, Rose Byrne, and Gabriel Byrne all shared selfies with signs of support for women in Irish theatre, with Nicole Kidman's message written on a bat, and captioned 'Nicole Kidman goes to bat for #WakingTheFeminists'.[9] Similar photographs with signs were shared by the all-female cast of *Henry V* from St Ann's Warehouse, New York, by Belarus Free Theatre, New Dramatists in New York, and by numerous arts workers in Ethiopia, shared by Lemn Sissay. Further messages were shared from directors John Tiffany, Phyllida Lloyd, Wim Wenders, Yaël Farber, and Vicky Featherstone, and from Sylvia Pankhurst's grandson, Alula. While the first event featured a list of speakers from across the Irish theatre industry, the second and third events included speakers from other industries including, film, journalism, comedy, technology, advertising, archives, the defence forces, and the trade unions. The final event also included

---

[9] https://twitter.com/tanyadean/status/665261266735337473.

prominent Irish activists including Micheline Sheehy-Skeffington, Sinéad Burke, Rory O'Neill, and Colm Burke; international theatre makers including Emma Rice and Susan Feldman; and international feminist activists, Mona Eltahawy and Eve Ensler. Speakers at the events approached the concerns of the campaign from a range of perspectives, traversing age, occupation, sexuality, race, geographical location, ability, and gender.

The campaign received widespread press coverage across the national newspapers in Ireland, with the first event in particular covered on all major news and current affairs programmes on national television and radio. It also featured in many of the main publications in the UK and was discussed in theatre and feminist blogs and podcasts. Helen Meany of *The Guardian* credited the campaign with fostering 'a new awareness, impossible to unlearn, of how power is exercised on stage and off' (2018). For RTÉ's Brainstorm, Mary Moynihan of TU Dublin described the campaign's impact as 'seismic' and highlighted 'the collective empowerment of women to challenge inequality and those in power and to ask the deeper questions of how women are viewed and treated in the theatre world and in society as a whole' (2018). Maggie Armstrong of the *Irish Independent* described the campaign as displaying 'supremely progressive, warm-hearted, tough love' (2016), while Una Mullally of *The Irish Times* designated its 'modern act of rebellion' as the missing ingredient from 'the carefully planned centenary commemoration' (2016). Lian Bell was awarded the Judge's Special Award at *The Irish Times* Irish Theatre Awards in 2016 for her work on the campaign, and #WakingTheFeminists were the first ever international recipient at the Lilly Awards in New York. At the award ceremony in 2016, Lisa Tierney-Keogh gave her #WakingTheFeminists necklace to Gloria Steinem.

The remarkable success of the campaign was mirrored by the extraordinary oversight of the Abbey in compiling its 2016 programme. One of the reasons why 'Waking the Nation' provoked such vociferous backlash was due to the fact that its purpose was to mark the centenary of the 1916 rebellion as part of a broader decade of commemorations (2012–23), which observed the centenaries of a turbulent period in Irish history that had culminated in civil war in 1922–23. Much of the focus of the centenary celebrations was on women's roles in these pivotal events, which had been systematically erased from history during decades of conservative Catholic government in the twentieth century. Ciara Murphy argues that this meant that 'the Abbey Theatre's commemorative programme was not only out of touch with society, but also with one of the overall focuses of the nationwide centenary programme' (Murphy, 2023). Miriam Haughton has also shown how the reaction to the Abbey's 1916 programme was fed by histories of active discrimination against women that are 'inextricably linked with the formation of the state as well as national

institutions' (Haughton, 2018: 354). Drawing a link between the literal airbrush-
ing of women like Elizabeth O'Farrell from photographs of the Easter Rising,
Haughton argues that '[i]t is this strategic erasure of women that became central
to the agenda of #WTF' (Haughton, 2018: 349). The centenary commemorations
were saturated with the historical legacy of the Rising, which acted not only as
a reminder of the ideals of the insurrectionists that the Republic would guarantee
'equal rights and equal opportunities to all its citizens' but also of the failure of the
State to fulfil this guarantee.[10] The place of women in relation to the founding of
both the national theatre and state will be discussed further in Section 1.

The second contributing factor to the intense scrutiny faced by the Abbey lies
in the close fiscal relationship between the national theatre and the state.
Founded by Lady Augusta Gregory and WB Yeats in 1904, the Abbey's early
years were marked by a repertoire in which the national identity was imagined
and interrogated. In 1925, it became the first state-subsidised theatre in the
English-speaking world. The financial support of the theatre from public monies
was central to the argument put forth by #WakingTheFeminists, which
demanded that publicly funded theatres be held accountable for how that
money was being disproportionately distributed to fund men's art. The Arts
Council/An Chomhairle Ealaíon is the primary funder of subsidised theatre in
Ireland, with the Abbey Theatre typically receiving about half of the Arts
Council's total theatre budget. In 2015, the Abbey's grant was €6.2 million,
more than seven times the amount awarded to the second-best funded theatre,
the Gate Theatre, which received €852,250 that year.[11] But the funding for the
'Waking the Nation' programme came directly from the Department of Arts,
Heritage and the Gaeltacht after an unsuccessful application by the Abbey for
funding from the Arts Council through an open call (Deegan and Mackin,
2015). Fiach Mac Conghail, who was at the time also a Senator in Seanad
Éireann, the upper house of the Oireachtas (parliament), negotiated directly
with the Department for an additional €500,000 to fund 'Waking the Nation'
(Deegan and Mackin, 2015). The extent of funding already awarded to the
national theatre, and the fact that it was able to secure additional funding for
a programme that had already been rejected from an open call by the Arts
Council, suggested enraging levels of entitlement and privilege.

#WakingTheFeminists' success derived not only from the commitment,
expertise, and tenacity of its organisers but also from fortunate circumstances,
like the timing of Mac Conghail's holiday, which were advantageous for the
establishment of the movement. Because by 2015, the popularity of the women's

---

[10] www.gov.ie/en/publication/bfa965-proclamation-of-independence/.
[11] www.artscouncil.ie/funding-decisions/?Artform=Theatre&Fund=Regularly%20funded%
20organisations&Year=2015#search.

movement had risen to the point where feminism had 'undeniably *become* popular culture', the generation of support for the campaign benefitted from the social prestige associated with such causes (Banet-Weiser and Portwood-Stacer, 2017: 884). Many theatre workers had been deeply involved in the recent Irish campaign to legislate for same-sex marriage, the success of which had not only whetted the appetite for further systemic change but provided important campaign experience that would prove invaluable for #WakingTheFeminists. The timing of the 'Waking the Nation' launch was also an auspicious moment as the theatre sector was on the cusp of transformation. Mac Conghail's eleven-year tenure as Director was coming to an end, and there was enormous excitement about his successors, Neil Murray and Graham McLaren, of the National Theatre of Scotland. The retirement of Michael Colgan from his decades-long reign at the helm of the Gate Theatre was also widely anticipated. The expectation of imminent changes in leadership at the two biggest Dublin theatres was augmented by a workforce that, since funding cuts in 2009, was mostly sustaining careers without the backing of the major funded companies. The combination of the knowledge that the existing directors' eras were at an end, with the majority of artists already working outside the patronage of cultural institutions, meant that the fear of repercussions for speaking out, which had silenced dissenting voices in the past, was greatly reduced. In short, the atmosphere was ripe for change.

While the response to the 'Waking the Nation' programme began on Facebook, it quickly moved to the more public facing, Twitter, which was adopted as the campaign's centralised communication stream. This move meant that anyone could follow the conversation as it was unfolding, while the platform's hashtags meant that the conversation could be centralised by theme, from which links to news articles, academic papers, videos, blogs, websites, and images could all be easily shared. Twitter, in 2015, was a fast-paced, text-based, micro-blogging site, ideally suited to capturing immediate responses to emerging events. In 2015, Ireland had the highest number of phone internet users in Europe, North America, and South America (Weckler, 2015) with about 26 per cent of Irish people over the age of fifteen using Twitter, and 92 per cent of Irish journalists using it every day (Coen, 2015). Twitter's 140-character limit[12] also made it perfect for short commentary on any topic, where wit, quips, and puns reigned supreme. These technical specifications of the site influenced the responses to 'Waking the Nation' to frequently feature satire, humour, and wordplay. With the sale of the platform to Elon Musk in 2022, and the subsequent restructuring and rebranding of the company to X, it has changed dramatically from that used by #WakingTheFeminists in 2015 and 2016. Changes to verification, authentication,

---

[12] Increased to 240 characters in 2017, and 25,000, for paid users, in 2023.

and moderation procedures dramatically altered the tenor of the site's contents after Musk's acquisition, which means that Twitter in 2015, while not without problems, was considerably more amenable for feminist campaigns than it is today.

The centrality of social media to #WakingTheFeminists aligns it with the dominant trend of fourth-wave feminism, which has seen a return to the consciousness-raising of the second wave mediated by digital technologies. Elasaid Munro describes how the shift online, which defines the fourth wave, has 'created a "call-out" culture, in which sexism or misogyny can be "called out" and challenged' (Munro, 2013: 23). The dramatic shift to calling out sexist and misogynistic cultures, which had hitherto been generally suffered as inevitabilities, typifies the kind of breaking point Sara Ahmed describes as a 'feminist snap' (Ahmed, 2017). The snap represents a critical moment in which building tension reaches a point of strain and fractures; it is 'the basis of a feminist revolt' (Ahmed, 2017: 210). The coining of the #WakingTheFeminists hashtag displays the kind of humorous punning typically seen on Twitter, but it was also a retort to Mac Conghail and the Abbey Theatre that released some of the growing anger back towards them. As Ahmed surmises: 'a hashtag can be snap' (Ahmed, 2017: 239). Prudence Chamberlain resists the wave narrative but notes with regard to feminism that 'particularly notable surges might be related to an increase in feeling, or an especially intensive affective period' (Chamberlain, 2017: 9). The concentrated release of pent-up emotion that happens at the point of fracture has frequently been channelled into online campaigns characterised by their affective intensity. In particular, Kay and Banet-Weiser note that the 2010s saw 'an extraordinary new visibility of women's anger—we might even say feminist anger—in public discourse and popular culture' (2019: 604). However, in the case of #WakingTheFeminists, the quick shift to in-person organising meant that this campaign was not simply a cathartic release of rage but an intentional effort to make tangible changes to how Irish theatre operates. Online social justice movements have frequently been dismissed as 'slacktivism', meaning 'activism for slackers' (Gerbaudo, 2012: 7), which entails simple actions like signing an online petition or adding a filter to a profile picture in a 'risk-free performance of virtue-signaling' (Clark-Parsons, 2022: 70). What made #WakingTheFeminists different was its strategic use of social media to generate public backing for a research-informed, data-driven campaign run predominantly by a team of highly skilled theatre producers.

Those involved in the campaign came from across the arts sector in Ireland, with its personnel changing with the evolving needs of the campaign over the course of the year. Led by Campaign Director, Lian Bell, they were anchored by a core group· of organisers, including Anne Clarke (Producer of

Landmark Productions), Tanya Dean (freelance dramaturg and theatre academic at National University of Ireland, Galway), Sarah Durcan (General Manager of Science Gallery International, previously theatre producer), Kate Ferris (freelance producer and teacher at The Lir Academy), Maria Fleming (theatre programmer at The Ark), Róise Goan (freelance producer), Niamh Ní Chonchubhair (Programme Manager and Producer at Axis, Ballymun), Dairne O'Sullivan (freelance PR and Press manager), Lynne Parker (Artistic Director of Rough Magic Theatre Company), Lisa Tierney-Keogh (playwright), and Caroline Williams (freelance producer). In the week preceding the first event, a venue had already been secured for the second public meeting 'Spring Forward', which took place at Liberty Hall in Dublin on International Women's Day, 8 March 2016. 'Spring Forward' offered an opportunity for theatre organisations to respond to the campaign and in addition to further testimonies, included presentations by Kate Ferris on the unique circumstances of women working in technical theatre, and by Sarah Durcan and Dr Brenda Donohue on unconscious bias. The movement's year of campaigning concluded back at the Abbey Theatre with the final event 'One Thing More' on 14 November 2016, which featured short speeches on the one remaining thing people wanted to change, and a presentation of provisional research findings from #WakingTheFeminists' impending report. Smaller events also took place on 6 January to mark Nollaig na mBan (Women's Christmas) and on 25 June for Feminist Midsummer, among #WakingTheFeminists branches in Belfast, Cork, Carlow, Galway, Kilkenny, Kildare, Kerry, Inis Oírr, Sligo, and New York.

Originally published on 8 November 2015, the campaign's objectives for every publicly funded theatre organisation were:

1. A sustained policy for inclusion with action plan and measurable results
2. Equal championing and advancement of women artists
3. Economic parity for all working in the theatre[13]

#WakingTheFeminists also published a list of nine recommendations for organisations, including recommending the introduction of gender equality policies and diversity policies with implementation plans; commitments to gender-balanced board membership; publication of gender statistics; commitments to re-evaluations, equity assurances, and public transparency of pay scales; a re-evaluation of the varied implications of parenthood and the introduction of practical supports for parents; the introduction of robust sexual harassment and dignity at work policies for both staff and contract workers; and a commitment to good quality unconscious bias training with a person

---

[13] www.wakingthefeminists.org/objectives-recommendations/.

trained and responsible for monitoring gender balance and diversity in every department.[14] The recommendations were followed by the distribution of 'Lian's List' at the 'One Thing More' event that contained seventy practical actions to combat sexism and unconscious bias in theatre, with steps 17–22 illustrating the pragmatic nature of the advice:

17 Make a commitment. Quotas and targets may work for you.
18 Make it public.
19 Stick to it.
20 Set a time frame for progress on gender equality.
21 Make it public.
22 Celebrate and mark when it happens.[15]

At the end of the campaign, #WakingTheFeminists gave a copy of Iris Bohnet's *What Works: Gender Equality by Design* to leading theatre organisations in Ireland. These campaign objectives reflect Bohnet's advice that 'replacing intuition, informal networks, and traditional rules of thumb with quantifiable data and rigorous analysis is a first step toward overcoming gender bias' (2016: 15). The steps detailed in 'Lian's List' build on the evidence that having targets, deadlines, and an awareness that people are watching make commitments to gender equality more likely to be adhered to. Both #WakingTheFeminists' recommendations and 'Lian's List' reflect the awareness within behavioural economics that systemic change is required to address the biases that cause gender inequality. Bohnet articulates that 'this is the very promise of behavioural design; it can change behavior by changing environments rather than mindsets' (Bohnet, 2016: 61). The campaign's research-informed strategy, which focussed on structural change rather than justifying women's worth as artists, makers, and workers, was paramount to its success.

#WakingTheFeminists' success also derived from the widespread support of the campaign's objectives, and its first achievement became clear on 30 August 2016, when the Abbey published its 'Eight Guiding Principles for Gender Equality'. This publication was welcomed as a template for the broader theatre community and was followed on 20 December by the first meeting of the Gender Policy Working Group. The group comprised initially five, and later, ten, leaders of theatre organisations and was created to collectively generate gender policies for each organisation.[16] A further significant milestone was the call by the Minister for Arts in March 2017, for all national cultural institutions

---

[14] www.wakingthefeminists.org/objectives-recommendations/.

[15] www.wakingthefeminists.org/take-action/.

[16] Initially comprising representatives from The Lir Academy, The Everyman, Abbey Theatre, Cork Midsummer Festival, and The Corn Exchange, they were later joined by Druid, Gate

to have gender polices in place by 2018, thus signalling the movement's reach beyond theatre and across the broader arts sector. #WakingTheFeminists' activity culminated on 7 June 2017 with the launch of their research findings, *Gender Counts: An Analysis of Gender in Irish Theatre 2006–2015*, which presented percentages for female representation across key artistic roles in the top ten funded Irish theatre organisations and found women to be 'poorly represented' in 'every role except Costume Designer' (Donohue et al., 2017: 7). The report's stark findings were greeted with astonishment and prompted a general resolve within the industry to do better.

This Element positions #WakingTheFeminists as a form of data feminism due to its combined use of qualitative and quantitative data throughout its campaign. Inspired by Donna Haraway's notion of feminist objectivity as situated knowledge (1988: 581), D'Ignazio and Klein define seven core principles of data feminism, which are: to examine power, challenge power, elevate emotion and embodiment, rethink binaries and hierarchies, embrace pluralism, consider context, and make labour visible (D'Ignazio and Klein, 2020: 17). Through its strategic use of data, #WakingTheFeminists distinguished itself from previous initiatives to address gender inequality in Irish theatre, including the establishment of The Women Playwrights Forum in 1991, Glasshouse Productions' festivals in 1992 and 1993, and the backlash to the Abbey Theatre's 'abbeyonehundred' programme in 2003. Section 1 will show how the dual histories of women's marginalisation in Irish theatre and numerous attempts to protest this marginalisation led to the snap that prompted the #WakingTheFeminists movement.

Contextualising the movement within two dominant strands of twenty-first century feminism, networked feminism and data feminism, this Element will analyse how the campaign's multi-faceted approach was essential to its success. Networked feminism brings together the defining elements of #WakingTheFeminists' campaign, which included activism on social media and in-person events, both of which facilitated connections between dispersed groups based on a shared emotional reaction to a specific event. Aristea Fotopoulou defines networked feminism as 'a form of contemporary political action that is characterised by complex connectivity and which operates at the intersections of online and offline, and across campaigning activities, feelings, and people' (Fotopoulou, 2016: 49). For #WakingTheFeminists, the connections facilitated by social networks enabled the collective expression of indignation at the disparity of the Abbey Theatre's 2016 programme. This resulted in the creation of an affective public, which is a public formation 'rendered into being

---

Theatre, Fishamble: The New Play Company, Rough Magic Theatre Company, and Dublin Theatre Festival.

through emotive expressions that spread virally through networked crowds' (Papacharissi, 2015: 133). The creation of this public led to an outpouring of testimonies detailing experiences of misogyny and sexism in Irish theatre, which formed an impromptu dataset that catalogued the history that had led to the collective snap. Section 2 explores how the preservation of this data on coordinated social channels and a dedicated website, and its use at the live events, was critical in charging the movement with the affective energy that drove it from social media and into collective organising.

The twenty-first century is quickly becoming the century of data. Driven by increased levels of mobile phone usage, the infiltration of smart technologies into household appliances, and advances in a huge variety of surveillance technologies, vast quantities of data are being captured by governments and organisations and used to structure daily life. Section 3 analyses how the publication of quantitative statistics by activist groups like #WakingTheFeminists helps to provide proof of systemic discrimination by shifting the perspective from subjective statements to objective data. This use of quantitative statistics will be contextualised in relation to similar projects by Emily Glassberg Sands (2009) in the USA and a variety of reports in the UK as part of a growing trend of using counting as a key tool for exposing gender inequalities. In Section 4, the impact of #WakingTheFeminists' campaign will be shown to have penetrated throughout the Irish arts sector, significantly influencing both policy and cultural changes. Among the outcomes of its campaign have been the creation of interventions to support freelance workers who experience bullying and harassment, the establishment of numerous groups advocating for better treatment for mothers and artists in a variety of disciplines, as well as interventions to increase the racial and ethnic diversity of Irish theatre. #WakingTheFeminists' remarkable achievements derive from its rapid implementation strategy, evidence-based approach to addressing gender bias, and some luck encountered along the way. In a short space of time, it made an extraordinary impact on the Irish arts sector and, by challenging its structure, has also affected its culture.

1 'Them the Breaks': Attitudes Towards Women in Irish Theatre

At the first public meeting, Eleanor Methven, co-founder of Ireland's first women's theatre, Charabanc Theatre Company, introduced herself as a 'chronic insomniac'. 'I have been awake since about 1976', she quipped (#WakingTheFeminists, 2015a). Citing a statement she had made in 1983 on the founding of Charabanc, Methven recalled: '[W]e were frustrated by the lack of good roles for women and decided we'd have to write them ourselves. We were tired of playing somebody's wife, somebody's girlfriend, somebody's sister, we wanted to be this somebody' (#WakingTheFeminists, 2015a). With exasperation, she then relayed a statement issued by Jo Cummins of Moonfish Theatre Company a week previously: '[F]rustrated by the lack of good roles out there for women, we knew we'd have to set up our own company and write the material ourselves. Roles where we could play more than merely the female appendage for the male protagonist.' '32 years in between', Methven fumed, 'any wonder I'm desperate for some sleep' (#WakingTheFeminists, 2015a).

At the 'Spring Forward' event in Liberty Hall, Caroline Williams commented that 'Waking the Feminists has moved like lightning over the last four months, but it has also taken decades' (#WakingTheFeminists, 2016a). #WakingTheFeminists was not the first attempt to address the under-representation of women on the Irish stage but was preceded by a historical legacy of feminists holding the establishment to account for the state-sanctioned mistreatment, marginalisation, and abuse of Irish women in public and private, as well as a cultural critique of a literary and theatrical tradition that represented women as metaphors, mothers, and muses. The histories of women's battle for equality in Irish theatre were evident throughout the campaign, and this section will review some of the most significant challenges to Irish theatre's androcentrism in the two decades preceding #WakingTheFeminists' protest. The analysis reveals that such feminist interventions appear to emerge roughly every ten years. The first flurry of activity occurred between 1991 and 1993 with The Women Playwrights' Forum and *There Are No Irish Women Playwrights! 1* and *2*, addressing the lack of visibility of plays by women by staging them as readings, compilations, and productions. Ten years later, in 2003, the backlash to the Abbey Theatre's centenary programme prompted criticisms in the national press of the low representation of women in 'abbeyone-hundred', in particular, the lack of a production of Lady Gregory's work. Ultimately, the progress made in increasing the numbers of women's plays being programmed in the wake of these events fell far short of parity, and it is this history that fuelled the feminist snap experienced by Bell in 2015. Ahmed describes the feminist snap as seeming sudden, 'but the suddenness is only apparent; a snap is one moment of a longer history of being affected by what you come up against' (Ahmed, 2017: 190). Two histories were palpable throughout the campaign. The first, a history of rejections, absences, and disappearances, fuelled the anger directed at the Abbey and the wider theatre community. The second, a history of interventions, of humour, and of hope, was palpable through the present bodies of women like Methven, Williams, and many others who had spearheaded the feminist charge in the past.

The election of Ireland's first female President, the prominent feminist activist, Mary Robinson, in December 1990 marked a turning point in Irish feminism, which was accompanied by a simultaneous rise in the prominence of women writers and an intensification of feminist critiques of the canon. In the #WakingTheFeminists-inspired essay collection, *Look! It's a Woman Writer!*, Éilís Ní Dhuibhne states: 'I believe the change regarding gender representation which has occurred in the field of literature to be more revolutionary, profound and historically significant than anything else that has happened in the closing decades of the twentieth century' (Ní Dhuibhne, 2021: 14). Eavan Boland described the revolutionary shift in poetry as one in which 'over a relatively short time – certainly no more than a generation or so – women have moved from being the subjects and objects of Irish poems to being the authors of them' (Boland, 1989: 6). The objectification Boland refers to was an inheritance from Irish-language poetry, in which a centuries-old nationalist tradition had fixed the image of Woman as a helpless captive awaiting a liberator (often a son) to free her. Dubbed Róisín Dubh or Cathleen Ní Houlihan, the woman in the traditional *aisling* (vision poem), acted as a cipher for the oppressed nation under colonial rule. This iconography became fused with venerated Roman Catholic figures like the Virgin Mary and Saint Thérèse of Lisieux, as well as the revered mothers of Irish freedom fighters, such as Margaret Pearse,[17] to iconise Irish womanhood in terms of purity and self-sacrifice, as mother and muse.

The impact of this legacy on the woman writer was the subject of vehement critique in the late twentieth century, with Eavan Boland making the critical point that 'Irish poems simplified women most at the point of intersection between womanhood and Irishness. [...] The nation as woman; the woman as national muse' (Boland, 1989: 13). This observation is particularly pertinent when considering that the 'Waking the Nation' season was designed to reflect on the impact of the Easter Rising, which was described as a 'poets' insurrection' (Kiberd, 1995: 285) due to the deep connections between the arts and revolutionary activity in the years preceding 1916, and the involvement of many of the insurrectionists with both the Abbey Theatre and the Theatre of Ireland (Morash, 2002: 152). Through numerous plays, poems, and prose, often written by the Rising's leaders, the rebellion was fuelled by myths of a country waiting for brave men to sacrifice their lives for its freedom. This myth is succinctly realised in the allegorical 1902 play, *Cathleen Ní Houlihan*, by Lady Augusta Gregory and W. B. Yeats, in which an old woman (Cathleen) seeks help to retrieve her four green fields (representing Ireland's four provinces) from the strangers in her house (signifying the foreign colonisers). Men in the play are promised immortality in exchange for their help in banishing the intruders: 'They shall be remembered for ever' (Yeats, 1991: 10), and Yeats himself

---

[17] Pearse encouraged her two sons, Willie and Patrick, to fight in 1916 and invoked their sacrifice publicly following their deaths. She is memorialised in Patrick Pearse's poem 'The Mother' (1916).

suggested that the play had inspired the rebels of 1916.[18] Performed on the Abbey Theatre's opening night in 1904, the play cemented the iconography of 'the nation as woman; the woman as national muse' within the national theatre's legacy. The centrality of this metaphor to the 1916 Rising, and the importance of the Rising itself in sparking the final movement towards independence, created a stifling symbolic inheritance with which women in Ireland would wrestle throughout the twentieth century.[19]

The framing of women as inert icons continues in the Abbey Theatre's marketing where an image of the warrior queen Maeve, originally designed by Elinor Mary Monsell in 1904 and reimagined by Steve Doogan in 2024, forms the centrepiece of the company's logo.[20] This inheritance was also reiterated in the promotional video for the 'Waking the Nation' programme in which the words of Helena Moloney, the Abbey Theatre actress who fought in 1916, were read by a cast of women (Abbey Theatre, 2015). The video provoked the same criticism as the design of the 'abbeyonehundred' programme, which had featured a prominent image of Marina Carr 'with a halo of male writers around her', despite the comparative inconspicuousness of her work in the season (Mulrooney, 2004). The marketing surrounding that programme also 'focused a great deal of attention on Lady Gregory's life and work' yet the representation of both her and Carr's work 'on the stage did little to realize the company's boast of "artistic and social inclusiveness" advertised in the brochure' (Maples, 2011: 103). Melissa Sihra described the 'abbeyonehundred' programme as 'an example of the symbolic centrality and subjective disavowal of women throughout Irish theatre past and present' (Sihra, 2018: 2). In both 'abbeyonehundred' and 'Waking the Nation', women were visually prominent in the announcements, but their work was materially unobtrusive in the programme. Icons and emblems, not writers and makers.

According to Victoria White, 'When Mary Robinson was elected in 1990 Irish women danced in the streets, because we knew that the shadowy Cathleen had been replaced by a flesh and blood woman' (White, 1993: 29). It was in this spirit of optimism that a series of feminist interventions took place in the early 1990s in an attempt to bring the stories of flesh and blood women onto Irish

---

[18] In 'Man and the Echo' (1939), Yeats wrote, 'Did that play of mine send out / Certain men the English shot?'

[19] Although the rebellion was unsuccessful, it ignited a surge in support for independence which, following the Irish War of Independence (1919–21) and the Irish Civil War (1922–23), was achieved for twenty-six counties of Ireland, now known as the Republic of Ireland. Six counties in the north of the country form the separate territory of Northern Ireland, which remains part of the United Kingdom. See also n.1.

[20] www.abbeytheatre.ie/stories-ideas-uproar-the-conversation-is-always-changing-at-the-national-theatre-of-ireland/.

stages. These interventions began in 1989, when a group of women comprising playwrights, Ivy Bannister, Leland Bardwell, Celia De Fréine, Clairr O'Connor, and Colette Connor, and administrator, Phyl Herbert, formed 'The Women's Playwrights Forum' to apply for project funding from the Arts Council to workshop and present rehearsed readings of five plays by women. In the letter confirming a grant of £2,000 was to be awarded, the Arts Council affirmed the application's assertion that 'a public performance for any playwright is very difficult but for women playwrights it would appear to be almost impossible' (Herbert, 2021: 304). In 1991, the Abbey Theatre's Literary Manager, Fintan O'Toole, and Artistic Director, Garry Hynes, agreed to host the readings in the Peacock Theatre (Herbert, 2021: 304). The readings were performed between 24 and 29 June,[21] and were followed by a discussion and Q&A chaired by Herbert in which there was general consensus that the Abbey needed to be 'more proactive' in its support of women playwrights (Herbert, 2021: 304). Despite this, Herbert observed that 'none of the women playwrights were offered the chance of a full production by the Abbey' (Herbert, 2021: 304). Having hosted the readings, advertised reductively in one poster as 'Women at the Peacock' (Herbert, 2021: 306), the Abbey Theatre reverted to the status quo. Reflecting on the event with resignation in 2015, Colette Connor remarked, '[I]n reality, the 'Plays by Women' turned out to be nothing more than a PR exercise.'[22] In this instance, the women had sourced the funding, written the plays, and organised the event. The theatre's input was minimal, but the reward was a visible event that created a perception that they were supporting female playwrights. The danger of such events is that they represent moral licensing which occurs when 'people respond to having done something good by doing more of something bad' (Bohnet, 2016: 53). In this case, the event created a feeling that the problem had been dealt with, which gave the theatre the license to return to its old routine. Much of the hope during this period rested on the fact that Garry Hynes would produce more plays by women. However, with her resignation two years later, Connor writes, 'whatever hopes and aspirations those present on the day may have entertained [...] those hopes and aspirations no longer applied to the Abbey' (Connor, 2009: 25).

The same year that 'Plays by Women' was presented at the Peacock Theatre, two additional incidents revealed the invisibility of women in the arts. The first was the publication of the three-volume *Field Day Anthology of Irish Writing* which created controversy due to its near total disregard of writing by women.

---

[21] www.wakingthefeminists.org/colette-connor/.
[22] www.wakingthefeminists.org/colette-connor/.

The second incident occurred when 'the American academic Claudia Harris went into a Dublin bookshop and asked for the shelf of Irish female playwrights. She was told: "There are no Irish women playwrights"' (Hayes, 2015). Spurred by these events, a young Dublin theatre company, Glasshouse Productions, decided to tackle the issues with more than a hint of irony. Glasshouse was an independent collective composed of director, Katy Hayes, producer, Caroline Williams, actor, Siân Quill, and actor and writer Clare Dowling. Provoked by the incidents mentioned earlier, Glasshouse presented 'Women Centre Stage' at the City Arts Centre in Dublin on International Women's Day in 1992. The event included a panel discussion, play readings, and a staged reading of twelve excerpts from contemporary plays by women devised by Caroline Williams, and playfully titled, *There Are No Irish Women Playwrights!* Noting that the Artistic Director of the Abbey Theatre at the time was Garry Hynes, Hayes articulated the company's disappointment that when the national theatre's 1993 programme was announced, 'there was the usual absence of female writers' (Hayes, 2015). Undeterred, the company presented a second festival in 1993, 'Acts and Reacts', which ran for six weeks at the Project Arts Centre, which was at that time under the directorship of Fiach Mac Conghail. Williams devised a second catalogue of plays by women from 1920 to 1970, *There Are No Irish Women Playwrights! 2*, and the festival also included new work, notably Emma Donoghue's sell-out *I Know My Own Heart*. The editors of *The Golden Thread: Irish Women Playwrights, 1716–2016* describe these festivals as marking 'a sea-change moment for contemporary Irish women playwrights' (Clare, McDonagh, and Nakase, 2021: 2). In an article published ten days after #WakingTheFeminists' first public event, Hayes wrote 'We truly believed we could change the world. Now that we had demonstrated how there were, in fact, plenty of female playwrights, surely they would all end up on the Abbey main stage?' (Hayes, 2015). Sadly, this was not the case, and in the same article Hayes described the emergence of #WakingTheFeminists as feeling 'like Groundhog Day' (Hayes, 2015).

In 2004, when criticism of the lack of female playwrights in the Abbey's centenary programme grew, Katy Hayes reflected on Glasshouse's achievements: 'We thought with a bit of agitation we could rectify the gender imbalance. [. . .] Instead of encouragement we got a lot of critical hostility [. . .] and general indifference' (Mulrooney, 2004). Critical feedback is inevitable when any artistic work is presented to an audience; however, in this instance, at least some of that critique stems from a group of predominantly male critics viewing plays about women as 'special interest'. Commenting on a male reviewer in *The Irish Times* who said of Clare McIntyre's *Low Level Panic*, 'Brothers, I think that this is one for the Sisters', Caroline Williams described it as 'a clear indicator to the company that there was a belief out there that plays by women were for women' (Williams et al., 2001: 137). #WakingTheFeminists avoided this issue by creating an argument based on a legal right to equal access to employment, rather than showing the evidence that women's work is worthy of production. The indifference Hayes described reflects the risk involved in presenting women's work in festivals, which can lead to implicit associations between plays by women, women's theatre companies, and, ultimately, audiences of women. Glasshouse's response to the apparent absence of Irish women writers from the public arena was to refute the argument. Their festivals proved that women have both a history and an active present in Irish theatre. However, the witty critique of these productions did not cut to the core of Irish theatre. The festivals did not present gender equality as a moral or legal gender discrimination issue, they did not structurally challenge the system, and the Irish theatrical establishment went back to its old tricks.

On 4 December 1994, 'The Abbey Debate' was the national theatre's attempt to respond to criticisms it had faced during its ninetieth anniversary year. Declan Gorman writes that 'the issues under discussion included not only gender but social exclusion, disability access, the closure of the education programme and a general sense that the Abbey had become isolated from the wider theatre.'[23] The issue of gender inequity in Irish theatre was put forward by Éilis Ní Dhuibhne, who remarked that '[t]he task of the age is to acknowledge the creative power of women in their own right, to accept and nurture the female artist, including that *rara avis*, the woman playwright' (Kilroy et al., 1995: 35). Ní Dhuibhne, whose *Dún na mBan Trí Thine* (The Women's Fort on Fire) had just been produced by the Abbey, states, 'The national theatre is doing itself and Irish society a disservice by not recognising the importance of staging plays by women' (Kilroy et al., 1995: 35). At that event, Gorman recalls that the Abbey's Literary Manager, Karin McCully, presented statistics that revealed that about 15 per cent of unsolicited scripts to the theatre were from women, and about 15 per cent 'of all the plays ever produced by the Abbey have been by women'.[24] This data attempts to suggest a correlation between the number of women approaching the theatre and the number of women programmed. Setting aside the fact that unsolicited scripts only make up a small percentage of all the plays ever produced by the Abbey, the proof of The Women's Playwrights Forum had already shown that simply bringing more plays to the theatre did not guarantee a production. While McCully used statistics at 'The Abbey Debate' to

---

[23] www.wakingthefeminists.org/declan-gorman/.
[24] www.wakingthefeminists.org/declan-gorman/.

defend the national theatre's position, it would be similar quantitative data that would ultimately force the theatre to face its gender issue in 2015.

The rise in the status of Marina Carr to the leading ranks of Irish playwrights in the late 1990s may have suggested that the situation was improving for women in Irish theatre. But when the Abbey Theatre announced its ambitious 2004 centenary programme, 'abbeyonehundred', its low representation of female playwrights generated controversy. Launched in November 2003, 'abbeyonehundred' was designed to mark the theatre's first hundred years through five seasons of work: The Abbey and Europe; The Abbey and New Writing; Summer at the Abbey; The Abbey and Ireland; and The Abbey on Tour. In total, the programme included eighteen[25] full in-house productions, ten play readings, five productions by visiting companies, and three touring productions. Two (11 per cent) of the eighteen full productions were by women. On the Peacock stage, Paula Meehan's play for young audiences, *The Wolf of Winter*, ran over the Christmas period of 2003–04, while Marina Carr's *Portia Coughlan* received a two-week run in the same space the following October. Every play programmed for the main stage in 2004 was written by a man. The absence of a production of any play by Lady Gregory, who co-founded the theatre and was one of its most prodigious playwrights, was noticeable. Her vast body of work was represented by a single staged reading of *Spreading the News* in the theatre's rehearsal room. It was presented as part of a double bill with George Bernard Shaw's *The Shewing Up of Blanco Posnet*, which means that 5 per cent of the plays presented as rehearsed readings were by women. The productions from visiting companies had between two and four performances each; just one of these was led by a woman (*Rain* by the Belgian company Rosas was choreographed by Anna Teresa de Keersmaeker). All of the touring productions were by men.

In the *Sunday Business Post*, Deirdre Mulrooney described the programme as representing 'the creative efforts and world-view of the Irish male' (2004) while Gerry Smith of *The Irish Times* described the scarcity of female playwrights as a 'miserable representation' (2003). Holly Maples notes that '[t]he paucity of work by female artists in the centenary was seen as a blatant disregard of the expansion of the role of women in Irish society' (Maples, 2011: 104). She quotes prominent Irish feminist activist, Ailbhe Smyth, who at the Abbey's

---

[25] The programme opened with Brian Friel's *Aristocrats* in November 2003, which was not part of the seasons. 'The Abbey and Europe' featured two productions. 'The Abbey and New Writing' featured five productions. 'Summer at the Abbey' featured four productions. 'The Abbey and Ireland' featured six productions. In September 2004, amid growing anxiety about the financing for the programme, two productions were postponed: Lennox Robinson's *Drama at Inish*, and Paul Mercier's *Smokescreen*.

'Memory and Repertoire' debate 'acknowledged her anger' over the programme and 'felt that "a whole generation of people" have been marginalized by this lack of the female perspective on the Abbey stage [and that] women, and other marginalized groups, are not just "forgotten", but "deliberately unremembered" by the Abbey Theatre and other cultural institutions' (Maples, 2011: 104). The fact that the gender disparity of the programme's playwrights wasn't even on the theatre's radar is evident in comments from then Artistic Director, Ben Barnes: "'It never occurred to me that we could be castigated for lack of commitment to women's writing," he says, adding that he has "no problem with how women are represented"' (Mulrooney, 2004). In his published diaries, in a vein similar to that expressed by Mac Conghail twelve years later, Barnes admitted he thought 'it was a non-issue and that [he] would only ever discriminate in favour of what [he] judged to be good plays, irrespective of the gender of the writers' (2008: 317). While many journalists addressed this issue following the programme launch, as the year got underway, it became increasingly clear that there were deeper issues urgently affecting the existence of the national theatre. The vast debt incurred by the centenary programme led to investigations that revealed serious financial issues at the theatre, effectively removing the issue of gender equality from the table. Dismissed and disregarded, gender inequality was deemed secondary to the pressing financial and governance concerns, rather than part of the problem.

Following the controversy around the Abbey Theatre's 2004 programme, particularly the lack of attention afforded to Lady Gregory in the commemorative year, no attempt to improve the representation of women at the theatre was made. While the 2005 programme included the production of a newly commissioned play by Shelagh Stephenson (the first female British playwright to be commissioned), in 2006 there were again no plays by women presented at the Abbey Theatre. In 2007, the Abbey produced new productions of Caryl Churchill's *A Number* and Marina Carr's *Woman and Scarecrow*, while in 2008, Belinda McKeon's short play *Two Houses* was produced by THISISPOPBABY in association with the Abbey at Project Arts Centre. It was, therefore, not until 2009, five years after the male-dominated 'abbeyonehundred' programme, before a new play by an Irish woman appeared at the national theatre: Marina Carr's *Marble*. While the situation improved in 2011 with four plays by women; out of a total of seventeen productions presented that year, this still only represented 23 per cent of the total programme. In 2013, Elaine Murphy became the first woman other than Marina Carr to have a play programmed on the Abbey's main stage in twenty-five years. The following year saw no Irish plays by women at the Abbey.

Table 1 shows that of the 149 plays presented between 2005 and 2015, just 20 (13 per cent) were by women.

Table 1 Plays by women at Abbey Theatre, 2005–15.[26]

Year	Total plays	Plays by women	Plays by women as % of total[27]
2005	12	1	8%
2006	13	0	0%
2007	11	2	18%
2008	16	1	6%
2009	12	2	17%
2010	12	3	25%
2011	17	4	23%
2012	10	1	10%
2013	16	3	19%
2014	16	1	6%
2015	13	2	15%
Total	**149**	**20**	**13%**

Source: Abbey Theatre Archive, www.abbeytheatre.ie/about/archive/

Of the forty-seven new plays produced during this eleven-year period, twelve (25 per cent) were by women. Of the fifty-two productions of existing plays during this eleven-year period, four (8 per cent) were written by women. Of the fifteen productions that had tours or revivals during this eleven-year period, one (7 per cent) was by a woman. Of the thirty-three plays presented at the Abbey by visiting companies, three (9 per cent) were by women. Of the twenty plays by women presented at the Abbey during this eleven-year period, only three (15 per cent) were presented on the theatre's main stage. Of the seven productions that received over 100 performances (including tours and revivals), one (14 per cent) was by a woman. No matter how the numbers are broken down, the answer remains the same: women did not feature significantly in any part of the national theatre's programme.

Although the representation of female playwrights at the Abbey Theatre during this period was very low, there were plays by women presented at the national theatre, predominantly on the smaller Peacock stage.[28] Under the Literary Directorship of Aideen Howard, female playwrights were commissioned, developed, and workshopped; however, there persisted a tendency towards ghettoisation when it came to the programming of their work. Twelve

---

[26] Including new plays (and new adaptations), new productions of plays from the canon, touring plays (including TYA), and short plays. It includes productions, co-productions, and plays produced in association with the Abbey as well as presentations of plays by visiting companies.

[27] Percentages have been rounded for clarity.

[28] The Peacock is a studio space with a seating capacity of 127.

(86 per cent) of the fourteen plays by women produced by the Abbey Theatre between 2005 and 2015 were presented in the smaller Peacock theatre, compared to twenty-six (31 per cent) of the eighty-three plays by men.[29] That the number of women represented improves the more the scale of the production is reduced is made evident from an analysis of play-readings at the theatre. The '20: Love' series in 2008, while not specifically aimed at women, had a significantly higher representation than that normally seen at the Abbey with three female and three male playwrights.[30] It was followed by the offensively titled 'The Fairer Sex' series of play readings in 2009, which appeared to confine the destiny of plays by women to public readings rather than promising a path to future productions. Contextualised by the previous ten years of programming, it becomes clear that 'Waking the Nation' was a manifestation of systemic disparity in the treatment of female playwrights at the Abbey. It is also clear that the frustration unleashed by that programme was the result of years of neglect and marginalisation of women's art at the theatre.

This history of marginalising and excluding women as playwrights and artists from the national theatre led to the feminist snap that Bell experienced in October 2015. As discussed in the Introduction, the feminist snap is a breaking point which Sara Ahmed describes as happening in 'a moment when the pressure has built up and tipped over' (Ahmed, 2017: 210). The launch of the 'Waking the Nation' programme crystallised latent memories of the theatre's historical discrimination against women into a moment of fury. However, the parallel history of feminist action in Irish theatre was also felt in this moment through figures like Charabanc's Eleanor Methven, Glasshouse's Caroline Williams and Katy Hayes, Belinda McKeon, who had been one of Ben Barnes' chief tormentors in her role as a journalist with *The Irish Times* in 2004, and many others who had spoken out against gender inequality in the previous decades. The moment of the snap therefore represents a compression of time in which the force of the past impinges on the present to cause a break, an 'unbecoming of something' (Ahmed, 2017: 188). The snap of course was not Bell's alone. It was a collective shattering of the illusion that women were content with the crumbs the institutions of Irish theatre were deigning to throw to them. In describing the feminist snap as political action work, Ahmed considers vigilantism as 'a feminist vigil, as a demand to stay awake to, or to wake up to, the violence directed against women. Snap: you need to wake up to what is already happening' (Ahmed, 2017: 208). The histories of many of the individual women who voiced their condemnation of the disparity of the

---

[29] Excluding tours, revivals, short plays, plays produced in association with the Abbey, and presentations of plays by visiting companies. Percentages have been rounded for clarity.

[30] Stacy Gregg, Nancy Harris, Paul Murray, Gary Duggan, Belinda McKeon, and Philip McMahon.

Abbey's programme attest to their awareness of Irish theatre's gender inequality issues. As individuals, they were already awake. The awakening that #WakingTheFeminists prompted was of the collective consciousness. It was a cultural wake-up call for the theatre community as a whole, and one that could not have been accomplished to the same degree without the digital tools of social networking.

2 Feminist Killjoys: From Connective to Collective Action

Fuelled by the collective snap experienced by Irish women in theatre in 2015, the outpouring of reactions to the 'Waking the Nation' announcement formed an organic, spontaneous, dataset on social media that captured the affective intensity of the growing #WakingTheFeminists movement. However, what had begun as ad hoc conversations on Facebook and Twitter, over time, came to be organised and documented through centralised accounts before being archived on the campaign's website. The impact of this move was to create a searchable dataset containing the criticisms of and commentary about the Abbey's programme, which made the evolution of the movement's development visible for artists, audiences, and the wider theatre community, including the Abbey's management. The speeches delivered by thirty women on the Abbey's main stage at the first meeting complemented the testimonies that had been shared online by embodying them in a durational presentation in which their affective impact was both personal and cumulative.[31] This section discusses the movement as a form of data feminism, by considering how the preservation of personal testimonies online and the presentation of women's experiences at the live events represented Donna Haraway's concept of feminist objectivity 'as positioned rationality' (Haraway, 1988: 590). It positions the initial silence-breakers as feminist killjoys and examines how the impassioned response to 'Waking the Nation' spread through online networks to create an affective public. Drawing on Sara Ahmed's account of how affect accrues from the circulation of signs, I will show how fear and shame moved between women as they shared their testimonies and back onto organisations like the Abbey Theatre. Laden with affect, the hashtag #WakingTheFeminists will be shown to have amassed a range of qualitative data that empowered the move from connective to collective action.

The snap experienced by women working in theatre in Ireland arose amid a wave of social justice movements in the 2010s that were facilitated by the

---

[31] Many of the testimonies that follow were initially posted on private Facebook accounts, screenshots of which were then shared by Lian Bell on Twitter, before being uploaded to the #WakingTheFeminists website. Where possible, I have referenced the website testimony as the most stable reference point for other researchers.

organising capacities of social media. Much academic attention has been afforded to salient campaigns that emerged in the wake of the global financial crisis of 2008 and were fuelled by anger and resentment at economic and social inequality. In particular, the 2011 social movements of the Arab Spring, the *indignados* movement in Spain, and the global Occupy movement, utilised the organising capacities of social media to plan and document protests and uprisings in cities across Africa, Europe, and North America (see Gerbaudo, 2012; Castells, 2015; Papacharissi, 2015). Around the same time, a wave of online feminist campaigns, such as #EverydaySexism in 2012 and #BeenRapedNeverReported and #YesAllWomen in 2014, linked traditional consciousness-raising techniques, public expressions of feminist anger, and the growing popularity of feminism in popular culture, in what has become known as 'hashtag feminism' (Clark-Parsons, 2022: 8–9). Kay and Banet-Weiser distinguish between the anger that fuelled the 2011 social justice movements, in which modernity 'failed to live up to its promises of democracy, equality and freedom' and the rage behind the feminist campaigns as being rooted in the fact that 'women were simply never made those same promises' (2019: 603–04). Orgad and Gill note that 'in the context of [. . .] post-feminism and neoliberalism, female anger, rage or complaint are systematically outlawed' and that 'the current moment [. . .] seems to represent a radical break' out of this repression (2019: 597–98). While I would temper this statement by acknowledging that for many groups of women, particularly women of colour, public expressions of anger continue to draw social reproachment, the late 2010s saw the suppressed rage of previous decades explode on social media, in the streets, and in popular culture. Kay describes this new outpouring of women's anger as representing 'a qualitative shift in the affective rules that govern public culture' (2019: 591). While historically, women's expressions of anger have been interpreted as the result of an innate hysterical nature, a child-like inability to self-regulate their emotions, or as signs of mental illness, in the 2010s, (some) public displays of (some) women's anger became increasingly accepted, if not legitimised, in the public sphere.

In this 'age of anger' (Kay and Banet-Weiser, 2019), social justice movements like the Arab Spring, the *indignados*, and Occupy were fuelled predominantly by a sense of indignation (see Gerbaudo, 2012: 14; Castells, 2015: 96; Papacharissi, 2015: 6). It is perhaps not surprising then that the spark behind Bell's Facebook post was, in her terms, a 'flurry of righteous indignation' (Bell, 2015). Indignation is a form of moral anger, defined as 'an affective reaction to a situation of injustice' (Knops, 2023: 9). Knops notes that it 'can be expressed on one's own behalf, or at the sight of an injustice committed to others whom we consider as ones *like us*', a process she describes as '*affective imitation*' (Knops, 2023: 9, italic in the original). Bell's anger was righteous because it was based on a blatant disparity that was plain to see; there is no ambiguity about the ratio 9:1. It was an anger expressed on behalf of those female playwrights and directors excluded from the 'Waking the Nation' programme, but also on behalf of female theatre workers and women in general. The connective element of indignation begins during affective imitation, when indignation is felt on behalf of a group. Because indignation is a 'public, talkative affect' (Knops, 2023: 9), it then extends beyond the individual when the same feeling resonates with others. This leads to the creation of affective publics, which, according to Papacharissi, are 'networked public formations that are mobilized and connected or disconnected through expressions of sentiment' (2015: 125). That platforms such as Twitter contribute to the shaping of such publics occurs because social media 'invite and transmit affect but also sustain affective feedback loops that generate and reproduce affective patterns of relating to others' (Papacharissi, 2015: 23). This, Papacharissi concludes, further reproduces affect, which she defines as 'intensity that has not yet been cognitively processed as feeling, emotion, or thought' (2015: 23). While Bell was consciously aware of the emotion driving her Facebook post, and able to identify it as 'righteous indignation', Papacharissi's definition of the transmission of affect on social media accurately captures the intensity and atmosphere of potentiality that characterised the early weeks of #WakingTheFeminists' campaign.

The righteous indignation expressed by Bell was echoed in many of the responses shared on social media, where they combined to create an affective public fuelled by outrage at the unfair representation of women in the Abbey's 2016 programme. In the immediate aftermath of the 'Waking the Nation' launch, Avril Ladybird tweeted 'no women playwrights in the @AbbeyTheatre 2016 programme, Waking the Nation. #wtn? More like #wtf'.[32] Displaying a mixture of incredulity and annoyance, evident in her use of punctuation, Fionnuala Gygax wrote 'Very disappointing/frustrating. No women playwrights or plays in Irish for 2016 …!?'[33] Liz Nugent's tweet revealed similar disbelief and frustration: 'I don't get it. Deirdre Kinahane [sic] is an EXCELLENT playwright ON THEIR BOARD and they won't produce her plays.'[34] Adopting a more sarcastic tone, Sarah David Goff tweeted 'Arts funding: nearly all. Female writers: nearly none. Great work everybody'.[35] The indignation expressed in these tweets fuelled the growing anger at the Abbey, with each response contributing to the accumulation of a public united by a common affective reaction. However, the anger displayed in these responses was not the anticipated reaction to 'Waking the

---

[32] https://twitter.com/Avril_LB/status/660184560177688577.

[33] https://twitter.com/GygaxFionnuala/status/659854716952817664.

[34] https://twitter.com/lizzienugent/status/659430968445546497.

[35] https://twitter.com/SarahDavisGoff/status/660120363532185600.

Nation'. As the last major programme launch of Mac Conghail's tenure, the 2016 programme was designed to be his swansong. Speaking about the possibility of a Broadway transfer of *The Plough and the Stars*, Mac Conghail commented, 'I can't think of a better high to end on' (Blake Knox, 2015b). This statement belies the celebratory tone that was expected for this significant programme. The initial public response to the launch of 'Waking the Nation' was positive; such occasions are designed to be celebratory and to generate excitement for the forthcoming season. The responses of Ladybird, Gygax, Nugent, and Goff were out of step with the anticipated and proscribed reaction to the event. They were not affected by it in the right way. Ahmed describes the feminist killjoy as 'an affect alien' who is 'not made happy by the right things' (Ahmed, 2017: 57). Indignation made these women killjoys because their appraisal of the 2016 programme was dominated by their perception of its unfair treatment of women. In this, indigna-tion may be the killjoy affect *par excellence* because the killjoy's starting point is the recognition that inequalities exist (Ahmed, 2017: 252). Therefore, the creation of this indignant public was the creation of a public of killjoys.

#WakingTheFeminists' emergence on social media in 2015 positioned it on the crest of a wave of hashtag feminism that flourished in the 2010s and reached a peak with #MeToo in 2017. The structure of the campaign's centralised communication stream, Twitter, contributed to the affective quality of the move-ment's development. The short length of posts and rapidity with which conversa-tions developed on Twitter in 2015 inclined users towards strong emotional reactions, with shock and anger featuring prominently. As emotive posts were shared using the hashtag, #WakingTheFeminists, each new contact brought new emotions that stuck to the hashtag, enriching its affective value as it circulated. To borrow Sara Ahmed's phrase, the more a hashtag circulates, the more affective it becomes (Ahmed, 2004: 45). Drawing on Ahmed's theory of the accumulation of affect, Kalim argues that the 'emotionality or affective value of hashtags increases during circulation' and that platforms like Twitter are 'affective sites where subjects, object, and their past histories come into play' (Kalim, 2023: 39). The call-out culture that characterised feminism in the 2010s was central to #WakingTheFeminists' campaign, and caused an increase in the affective value of the hashtag as organisations who failed to engage with the movement were held to account on Twitter. In the early days of the movement, Lian Bell maintained a focus on the Abbey Theatre, tweeting on 28 October: 'After @belindamckeon & @UnaMullally #nationaltheatreofmen comments, deathly silence from @AbbeyTheatre. Would love to hear their side.'[36] Bell was joined by others who held colleagues to account for not speaking up. Kate Ferris commented on

---

[36] https://twitter.com/lianbell/status/659444087804862464.

the absence of engagement from prominent theatre workers: 'Silence from the regular loud voices is currently speaking volumes #WakingTheFeminists #WakingtheNation.'[37] This sentiment was echoed by Louise White, who said: '[G]reat to see more men joining the conversation and standing with #WakingTheFeminists. Still a lot of silence out there.'[38] This strategy of holding individuals to account for not supporting the protest caused a disturbance, which is the aim of the killjoy (Ahmed, 2017: 251). By shaming others into publicly supporting the campaign, these tweets impacted the affective power of the hashtag, attaching it with a sense of danger. This sense of danger triggers further engagement as people follow to find out who will be outed next. It also attaches the accusatory tone to any tweet with the hashtag. When calling people out becomes a dominant strand in the conversation, any tweet with the same hashtag carries a trace of that narrative. Censure sticks to the hashtag, affecting everyone who reads it.

In providing testimonies, many women shared revisionist accounts of some of the affirmative action schemes the Abbey had been proud of. Olwen Fouéré wrote on Facebook: 'Ironically, one of the biggest insults in my view was when the Abbey has a season of "women playwrights" and called it "the fairer sex". Ugh.'[39] The memory of that programme and the way it was marketed prompted visceral reactions of nausea from other playwrights. Lisa Tierney-Keogh wrote: 'It turns my stomach when I think of that. It was a tiny, embarrassing morsel, a crumb', while Abbie Spallen revealed 'I was offered it and turned it down. Couldn't stomach it.'[40] The disgust felt by the women at the way they were being patronised, ghettoised, and sexualised by the season triggered feelings of sickness in their stomachs. Ahmed writes that 'disgust is deeply ambivalent, involving desire for, or an attraction towards, the very objects that are felt to be repellent' (Ahmed, 2004: 84). This mixture of attraction and repulsion is particularly apt for those who were part of the scheme, despite their aversion towards it. Ursula Rani Sarma shared: 'I was part of the Fairer Sex, I cringed at the title and I cringed at the fact that all the playwrights faces were plastered on the poster to advertise the event like a lovely girl competition.'[41] The verb 'to cringe' involves experiencing 'an inward shiver of embarrassment or disgust' ('Cringe', 2006). Embarrassment contains a feeling of shame, and disgust prompts the nausea described by Tierney-Keogh and Spallen. While some of this shame and the embarrassment that made Rani-Sarma cringe may have been self-directed, the act of cringing also happens on behalf of another. Róise Goan

---

[37] https://twitter.com/katerferris/status/661243138288304128.
[38] https://twitter.com/louisewhiteperf/status/661078166006534144.
[39] https://twitter.com/lianbell/status/660584075770650624.
[40] https://twitter.com/lianbell/status/660584075770650624.
[41] https://twitter.com/lianbell/status/660885261958692864.

described how, while sitting on the Abbey's board, she 'would cringe uneasily when the Director would point out that 4 plays produced in the previous year were by women'.[42] Goan's reasoning ran 'when the Abbey produces or presents up to 12 shows a year, should the fact that one third of them are by women be something we should celebrate?'[43] Shame is 'a painful feeling of humiliation or distress caused by the consciousness of wrong or foolish behaviour' ('Shame', 2006). However, Goan's cringe at the Abbey board meeting is caused by the consciousness of *their* foolishness. It is caused by the Director's absence of self-awareness, and Goan's total awareness of the inappropriateness of celebrating inequality. Throughout the online campaign, the shame and disgust felt by women interacting with the Abbey was returned onto the national theatre, which was made shameful and disgusting by their recollections.

The comments and testimonies posted by those women currently working in the theatre industry were not shared lightly. At the final public meeting, one year after the first event, Lian Bell said, 'I think back to this time last year when speaking up, proclaiming our opinions, and telling our personal stories felt, for some of us, dangerous. That we might lose too much.'[44] Throughout the testimonies shared online and from the Abbey stage, fear of the consequences of speaking out became a persistent refrain. This fear was attributed by many established artists to moments when they had occupied the role of the killjoy in the past. Noelle Brown recalled more than once being 'accused of being a lesbian man hater' when she confronted sexism in rehearsals rooms[45] while Sarah Jane Scaife relayed that those 'who couldn't compromise or keep our mouths shut went outside the institutions and made theatre wherever we could'.[46] That this move outside the houses of power was, in fact, a banishment was referenced by Gina Moxley, who remarked that '[w]omen with opinions or ambition are regarded as trouble [. . .] and are sidelined or blacklisted'.[47] These past experiences of killing joy in the rehearsal room created the fear expressed by many of speaking out. Ultimately, however, many also faced this fear with sarcastic humour. Lisa Tierney-Keogh remarked: 'When I was asked the other day if I was prepared for any backlash, my response was "what are they going to do? Not put my play on?"'[48] This sentiment was echoed by Ursula Rani Sarma, who asked, 'what is there to be afraid of? Of being left out? That ship has long sailed . . .'[49] The more that women referenced

[42] www.wakingthefeminists.org/roise-goan/.   [43] www.wakingthefeminists.org/roise-goan/.

[44] www.wakingthefeminists.org/lian-bell-one-thing-more-speech/.

[45] www.wakingthefeminists.org/noelle-browne-2/.

[46] www.wakingthefeminists.org/sarah-jane-scaife-public-meeting-speech/.

[47] http://www.wakingthefeminists.org/gina-moxley-public-meeting-speech-12-november-2015-2/.

[48] https://twitter.com/lianbell/status/661576268551450624.

[49] https://twitter.com/lianbell/status/661576268551450624.

the dangers of speaking out, and the more that they committed to relinquishing their fear of those dangers, the more affectively charged the hashtag became with a sense of that danger. Women were using the hashtag to expose truths about the sector that had been kept silent and this attached a sense of risk to the hashtag that made it compelling. 'Stickiness', writes Ahmed, 'involves a transference of affect' (Ahmed, 2004: 91). In sticking to the hashtag, the women's past fear of speaking out shifted onto theatre organisations that now feared the exposure of their own poor records of gender inequality. Paradoxically, abandoning their fear made the women fearsome, and the industry fearful.

Relinquishing this fear enabled many women to tell stories of their experiences at the Abbey. Their testimonies were critical to the growing dataset because they gave weight to the campaign by offering concrete evidence of the national theatre's disengagement with women. They provided fuel for the growing anger and offered solidarity, which prompted further people to come forward with their own stories. Director, Annie Ryan, wrote: 'I realised a few years ago that my yearly meetings on the top corridor, which I always enjoyed, were all instigated by me. So I stopped inviting myself and moved on to other conversations.'[50] In solidarity, Oonagh Murphy, a former resident Assistant Director at the Abbey, added: 'I too have banged my head quite a lot on that glass ceiling of the top corridor. [...] I too stopped sending emails to arrange meetings, and the meetings stopped.'[51] Writers reported similar experiences of engagement with the theatre that seemed futile from the start. Playwright, Alice Barry, remembered being 'called into the Artistic Directors office to be told that he had over programmed his final six months' and her play was being dropped in a year in which just one out of seventeen plays presented at the theatre was by a woman.[52] Ioanna Anderson, who described herself as 'one of Fiach Mac C's women commissions that "didn't work,"' said 'It was immediately clear they would not produce the play but they sat on it for three years without producing it or releasing it and me from our contract.'[53] Rosemary Jenkinson also described herself as 'one of the nameless women Fiach mentioned who had a commission with the Abbey that didn't "work out"'.[54] She recalled that 'there was absolutely no drive to put it on' and that shortly afterwards playwright, Frank McGuinness, said, 'I've heard this happening to loads of women writers at the Abbey'.[55]

---

[50] www.wakingthefeminists.org/annie-ryan/.

[51] https://twitter.com/lianbell/status/660892092697300992.

[52] www.wakingthefeminists.org/alice-barry/.

[53] Anderson also noted that her play had 'a love story between two middle aged women which the literary manager kept saying would make audiences uncomfortable'. www.wakingthefeminists .org/ioanna-anderson/.

[54] www.wakingthefeminists.org/rosemary-jenkinson/.

[55] www.wakingthefeminists.org/rosemary-jenkinson/.

McGuinness' comments testify to the fact it was common knowledge that the Abbey was 'a cold house for women playwrights' (Mulrooney, 2004). Each of these testimonies contributed weight to the dataset that increased its veracity. Any one of these anecdotes alone could have been dismissed as an isolated oversight, but the conscious collection of this data into an organised database revealed the pattern of systemic discrimination.

That this sense of an absence of interest by the theatre in producing work permeates the subconscious of writers under commission was articulated by Belinda McKeon who described the difficulties she faced when writing plays for the Abbey: '[I]t has always felt pointless, because at a deep level that I don't quite understand I've never truly believed that anything is going to happen with it.'[56] While rejection and disappointment are expected within the theatre industry, the picture that emerges from the repeated stories of women's engagement with the Abbey is one of disinterest and insincerity, of glass ceilings and closed doors. It is a picture painted most clearly in the story of Lynda Radley's experience with the Abbey. Speaking on the Theatremaker's Roundtable, at the Irish Women Playwrights and Theatremakers conference in 2017,

> Radley described flying from Scotland for a meeting with the Abbey Theatre. When she arrived at the theatre doors, she found them closed and locked – they had forgotten about her. Radley recalled the moment as emblematic of the larger ethos of theatre in Ireland for women artists: 'Here I am, knocking at a door that doesn't seem open to me' (Nakase, 2017).

The repetition of the metaphors of the closed door and the glass ceiling by leading artists in Irish theatre gave credence to claims that its culture was hostile for women. At the time of sharing, testimonies provided important evidence that women were not being given a fair hearing at the Abbey. Following the publication of the statistical data, these testimonies offered context and qualitative information about why women were not being programmed. Repeated rejection and a perception that the theatre did not support women was disabling for them creatively and discouraging them from engaging. D'Ignazio and Klein emphasise that 'you can only detect the pattern if you know the history, culture, and context that surrounds it' (D'Ignazio and Klein, 2020: 65). The specificity of these testimonies explicitly connected them to a particular institution at a specific time, and implied a host of contextual information about a programming culture that has been described as 'whim-ridden' (Hayes, 2015). The importance of not letting the numbers speak for themselves is that in the absence of context, a vacuum exists in which women are blamed for not submitting work to the theatre, or not submitting work that is good enough to programme, or that women writers or directors

---

[56] https://twitter.com/lianbell/status/660531233382887424.

simply do not exist. These testimonies refute all these arguments by revealing that women do exist, and have tried to engage, and have been programmed, but that a limit exists to how many times they will bang on a closed door before they walk away.

Indignation was the dominant emotion driving the early weeks of the campaign. The usefulness of the anger within indignation is that it generates energy that prompts action. Audre Lorde writes that 'anger expressed and translated into action [. . .] is a liberating and strengthening act of clarification' (Lorde, 1981: 8). For #WakingTheFeminists, this action began with the clear and deliberate organisation of criticisms and testimonies into a coherent online presence. The consequent creation of an affective public hinged on the affective power of posts shared with the hashtag, the strength of which prompted the move to collective action offline. The feminist snap that originally prompted the movement has been discussed in Section 1 as a fracture that happened as a result of an accumulated history of discrimination and marginalisation. The abruptness of this fracture is critical to Ahmed's conception of the snap, which she describes as 'a sudden quick movement' (Ahmed, 2017: 188). Bell's snap was followed by a speedy succession of events that led to the first public meeting. Like Bell's snap, the most important feature of that meeting was its temporality. However, in this case, it was not a 'sudden quick movement', but the comparatively slow progression of a live event that made it so powerful. The move from connective to collective action slowed the data down. According to D'Ignazio and Klein, 'Data feminism teaches us to value multiple forms of knowledge, including the knowledge that comes from people as living, feeling bodies in the world' (D'Ignazio and Klein, 2020: 73). At the first live event, thirty women took their place on the Abbey stage in a symbolic gesture of reclamation of the national theatre. O'Toole described this gesture as 'not only knowingly performative but also allied to performance in the theatrical sense; in taking to the Abbey stage the movement signalled consciousness of the power of representation, of the vital relationship between what is seen and what is believed' (O'Toole, 2017: 137). The live events offered the opportunity to situate these testimonies within the specific bodies of the attestors or their nominated speakers. Each of the speeches formed a piece of data that represented the specific experience of a particular individual. But patterns and echoes emerged between speakers and together, these testimonies represented the multifaceted perspectives of a group of women who agreed that there was a problem with gender inequality in Irish theatre. D'Ignazio and Klein use Elevator Repair Service's *A Sort of Joy (Thousands of Exhausted Things)* to demonstrate the impact of data presented as performance. In this performance, metadata about the artworks held by New York's Museum of Modern Art (MoMA) is presented durationally, as male performers say the name of male artists whose work features in MoMA's collection, while female performers say the names of female artists (D'Ignazio and Klein, 2020: 86–87). The names are pronounced in order of the frequency with which they appear in the collection, beginning with the Johns, the Roberts, and the Davids. Gradually the audience becomes aware of the performance's structure and the lengthy periods in which the female performers are silent. D'Ignazio and Klein describe how '[i]n this data performance, we do not see the overview first. We hear and see and experience each datapoint one at a time and only slowly construct a sense of the whole' (D'Ignazio and Klein, 2020: 87). It is the slowness of the revelation, which is learned through the experience of the performance rather than via didactic instruction, that makes it so powerful. At #WakingTheFeminists first live event, in particular, the experience of each individual testimony gradually culminated in a revelation of the scale of gender inequality in Irish theatre. Because in a durational experience such as this, '[w]e *feel* the gender differential, rather than *see* it' (D'Ignazio and Klein, 2020: 87, italic in the original), its impact is more visceral.

When women's testimonies are presented in isolation, they are easily dismissed as unfortunate anomalies. When they are presented successively, on stage, in an auditorium over the space of ninety minutes, they become evidence of a pattern. Patterns reveal problems to be systemic and are therefore much more difficult to dismiss. The affective impact of the live witnessing is felt bodily by the audience, with the weight of each speech accumulating over time. At the first public meeting, hearing the frustration of playwrights like Ursula Rani Sarma, Lisa Tierney-Keogh, and Ali White when confronted with the phrase 'there are no women playwrights' will gradually trouble the audience: 'we are right here, being produced, published, and academically studied throughout the world. Is there some sort of giant firewall surrounding Ireland that means our success is invisible to many within?'[57] Hearing Janet Moran talk about actors being '[o]bjects of desire or derision',[58] Gina Moxley describing how '[o]n a fundamental level we are not trusted',[59] and Noelle Brown speak about the casting couch, body shaming, and unequal pay[60] will have a cumulative impact on the audience members. While testimonies shared online may be viewed individually, the successive impact of hearing story after story in a theatre, or via a live stream, is more intense. Unlike a social media feed, 'presenting the dataset as a time-based experience makes the audience wait and

---

[57] www.wakingthefeminists.org/ursula-rani-sarma-public-meeting-speech/.

[58] www.wakingthefeminists.org/janet-moran/.

[59] http://www.wakingthefeminists.org/gina-moxley-public-meeting-speech-12-november-2015-2/.

[60] www.wakingthefeminists.org/noelle-browne-2/.

listen and experience' (D'Ignazio and Klein, 2020: 87). Hearing Pom Boyd announce from the floor that her experience with the Abbey forced her to withdraw from theatre, and that she now refers to herself as an 'ex-playwright' will have a greater impact because of the variety of stories of disdain, distrust, and diminishment that have preceded it (#WakingTheFeminists, 2015b). For those in attendance, or watching online, this moment would have prompted the dawning realisation that the voices that they have heard from the stage are those that survived the system. There are countless others, like Boyd, who have left the profession completely.[61] The importance of these live testimonies lies in the fact that 'activating emotion, leveraging embodiment, and creating novel presentation forms help people grasp and learn more from data-driven arguments, as well as remember them more fully' (D'Ignazio and Klein, 2020: 88). The slow revelation of speech after speech detailing instances of discrimination by leading theatre makers allowed the affective impact of their testimonies to amass while uncovering patterns of behaviour too common to ignore.

The rage that had fuelled the feminist fire online was palpable in the charged atmosphere of the live event. With Fiach Mac Conghail sitting in the middle of the auditorium, displays of anger from the stage ranged from Jen Coppinger's quiet seething as she recalled a career in which she responded to her own ambitions with the phrase 'Cop on!' to Mary Duffin's loud 'I'm mad as hell and I'm not going to take it anymore!' (#WakingTheFeminists, 2015a). Anger also manifested in metaphors of burning rage in many of the testimonies. Maeve Stone quoted from an interview with Marina Carr in which she talks about her play *By the Bog of Cats*. The description captures the affective intensity of #WakingTheFeminists' campaign: 'The rage in women is terrifying. [. . .] The rage comes out of being said no to just one time too many, where you should have been said yes to, if the world was fair. [. . .] If society is always saying no to you, that rejection has to go somewhere. It turns dark, and it erupts then.'[62] Olwen Fouéré and Kate Gilmore also drew on metaphors of fire to describe the movement, saying 'Huge thanks to Lian Bell who started the fire. Long may it burn!'[63] and 'Thank you to those who have ignited the flame. May it rage like an inferno.'[64] Each time the fiery rage is mentioned, its affective impact on the gathered assembly grows. Each time the women onstage reinforce each other's testimonies, the argument they are making is strengthened. Each data point adds

---

[61] Boyd's career has seen a revival since this moment. She has appeared as an actor in a number of plays at the Abbey Theatre since 2015. In 2018, her play *Shame* was produced at the Peacock as part of Dublin Fringe Festival.

[62] www.wakingthefeminists.org/maeve-stone/.   [63] www.wakingthefeminists.org/olwenfouere/.

[64] www.wakingthefeminists.org/kate-gilmore-public-meeting-speech/.

further proof that the problem is not individuals, but a culture of discrimination and exclusion.

In her Foreword to *Gender Counts*, Lian Bell wrote: 'This was not, of course, the first time these kinds of testimonies had been heard. [. . .] But this time was different. [. . .] This time we spoke as one, and were listened to' (Donohue et al., 2017: 5). The difference was in part due to the affective affordance of social media, which allowed women to make connections that linked their experiences and confirmed a culture of discrimination across Irish theatre. The coordination of qualitative data on social media, and its presentation at the live events, was critical to developing a body of evidence to support claims that gender bias was negatively affecting women's careers. While the accumulation of affect through the hashtag, #WakingTheFeminists, on Twitter helped to generate the affective intensity that drove the move from connective to collective action, the live presentation of testimonies solidified its impact in a concentrated, durational experience that amplified the impressions made by these testimonies and revealed their underlying patterns. The revelation of these patterns then created the impetus for quantitative research to confirm the intuitive knowledge that Irish theatre had been systemically favouring men in key creative roles for years.

3 Gender Counts: The Persuasive Power of Numbers

#WakingTheFeminists' final significant development was the procurement of funding from The Arts Council/An Chomhairle Ealaíon to commission a report into gender inequality in Irish theatre. Following the original impulse of Lian Bell's Facebook message, *Gender Counts: An Analysis of Gender in Irish Theatre 2006–2015* counted the number of women employed as writers, directors, and designers by the top ten funded theatre organisations in Ireland (Donohue et al., 2017). Significantly, it moved the argument from personal testimony to collective oppression, as the quantitative data provided proof of systemic discrimination against women in Irish theatre. This use of quantitative data emerges in the context of a wave of similar statistical reports, notably Emily Glassberg Sands' *Opening the Curtain on Playwright Gender: An Integrated Economic Analysis of Discrimination in American Theater* (2009) in the USA and Victoria Sadler's blogs in the UK. Drawing on the work of Theodore Porter (2020), this section will explore the affective impact of this quantitative data as the critical strategical development from previous gender equality initiatives. Its importance will be shown to derive from the persuasive power of numbers to appeal to reason and counteract claims of a meritocracy, while offsetting rebukes of emotionality or overreaction by the campaigners.

With hyper-connectivity emerging as the defining characteristic of twenty-first century life, data is fast becoming the century's most valuable resource. The 2010s saw an increase in the number and frequency with which statistical reports on gender inequality, in all areas of life, were being published. Yet this use of statistical data has its roots in the nineteenth century when the British colonial enterprise required the recording and measuring of huge quantities of data from around the world as a means of justifying as well as quantifying the empire. What Theodore Porter describes as the 'positivist mania for quantification' (2020: 20) emerged alongside social Darwinism and the eugenics movement, as much of the data generated was used to support beliefs in the superiority of certain races and classes of people over others. Gina Rippon outlines how the continued debate on the Woman Question in the nineteenth century meant that '[t]here was to be no stone unturned (or skull unexamined) in the hunt for the proof of women's inferiority' (Rippon, 2019). Proof is the operative word here, and the obsession with generating data was in service of making the belief in traditional gender roles irrefutable. D'Ignazio and Klein argue that this nineteenth-century eugenicist inheritance continues to influence modern statistics' 'belief in the benefit of cleanliness and control' of data (2020: 131). Despite these origins, an important shift happened in the latter half of the twentieth century when the same statistical methods began to be employed to prove the sexism and racism of governing institutions. Numeric data, in particular, are useful for feminist campaigns because they are seen as emotionless. When Sarah Durcan and Dr Brenda Donohue gave a presentation on existing research on unconscious bias and gender statistics at #Waking TheFeminists' second event, 'Spring Forward', they emphasised that the perspective of the conversation was switching to objectivity. Durcan invited the audience to 'peel away all the emotional stuff' while Donohue emphasised the integrity and utility of statistical information: 'The numbers are clear, honest, and informative. Let's use them' (#WakingTheFeminists, 2016b). Condensing the experiential knowledge shared as testimonies into statistical data does not, however, mean that the quantitative data is not affective, but its presentation in an abstracted form replaces the doubt of subjectivity with faith in objectivity.

In *Trust in Numbers*, Porter explains that quantification functions as a means of communication between people who do not know or trust each other by introducing objectivity through standardised measurements that eliminate the need for trust, and therefore the distance between communities (2020). Describing quantification as 'a technology of distance', Porter explains that 'reliance on numbers and quantitative manipulation minimizes the need for intimate knowledge and personal trust' (2020: xxi). For #WakingTheFeminists, quantification came in the form of statistics that supported the qualitative data already shared online and at the live events. Its function was to provide numeric proof that the under-representation of women in Irish theatre was widespread and persistent. 'Trust is inseparable from objectivity', Porter writes, '[b]ut the form of trust supporting objectivity is anonymous and institutional rather than personal and face to face' (2020: 214). As quoted in Section 2, Gina Moxley's testimony summarised the position of women in Irish society in terms of a fundamental absence of trust. For #WakingTheFeminists, statistics helped to express the subjective testimonies in terms of the proportion of roles occupied by women, thus making them objective, and therefore trustworthy. Because in most contexts 'objectivity means fairness and impartiality', the introduction of quantitative statistics, conducted by independent academic researchers, with a transparent methodology, meant that trust could be placed in the process, rather than in individuals (Porter, 2020: 4). Significantly, the quantitative abstraction enabled #WakingTheFeminists to articulate the problem faced by women in Irish theatre in a way that was transparent and immediately under-standable. In this, the movement differed from previous campaigns in which the problem was framed as one of perception, and the solution was to make plays by women more visible. The focus of these previous initiatives was on specific plays and playwrights, but #WakingTheFeminists' quantification of the gender disparity in Irish theatre shifted the focus onto theatre organisations. Plays and playwrights are not named in *Gender Counts*, but theatre organisations and figures for their representation of women are, and this abstraction moved the attention away from individuals and onto the system. This shift to objectivity does not mean that such data are not emotive. In fact, research by Kennedy and Hill finds that 'a wide range of emotions characterise engagements with diverse aspects of data and visualisations, which in turn demonstrates the importance of emotions in efforts to make sense of data' (Kennedy and Hill, 2018: 831). Emotions are not only important for engagement with data. When the data is designed to prompt changes in behaviour, its power to produce strong affects becomes essential.

The use of data by feminists as part of gender equality campaigns is not new; however, the ease with which statistical data can be generated from an array of accurate information sources online has led to a greater frequency in the produc-tion of quantitative reports on gender inequality in theatre in the last two decades. *Gender Counts* formed part of a growing trend of quantitative research on gender inequality throughout the 2010s. One of the most significant reports that influenced #WakingTheFeminists' research was Emily Glassberg Sands' undergraduate the-sis, which presented an economic analysis of gender inequality on Broadway (Glassberg Sands, 2009). This startling report found that while 'less than one-eighth of productions on Broadway are female-written' (105), female-written work on Broadway 'sells more tickets per week than its male-written counterpart' (101) and female-written productions on Broadway 'garner an estimated 18 percent higher weekly revenue than their male-written counterparts' (99). Glassberg Sands also found that:

> Scripts bearing female pen-names are deemed by artistic directors to be of lower overall quality and to face poorer economic prospects than otherwise identical scripts bearing male pen-names. [. . .] Female artistic directors, in particular, deem scripts bearing female pen-names to be poorer fits with their theaters. [. . .] The severity of the discrimination against female playwrights appears to be more pronounced for women writing about women than for women writing about men (2009: 104–05).

The report, which received media coverage in *The New York Times*, *Huffington Post*, *Vulture*, and elsewhere brought the reality of gender inequality in theatre to the public consciousness. It also established the power of quantitative analysis for exposing the discrimination faced by women in theatre in economic terms. This report was followed in 2015 by the establishment of *The Count*, 'an ongoing study that asks the question "Who is Being Produced in American Theatres?"' (Jordan and Stump, 2015). Its findings in the first iteration revealed a low proportion of women represented among the productions counted (20.3 per cent) and a particularly low proportion of productions written by American women of colour (3.4 per cent) (Jordan and Stump, 2015). However, this report also shows the power that producing such statistics can have. By the publication of the second report, which analysed the 2016–17 season, the percentage of American women of colour had almost doubled to 6.1 per cent, while the overall representation for women increased to 28.8 per cent.[65] These reports reveal both the trend for statistical data on gender representation in American theatre, and also the value that insights from statistical data can bring. The capacity to measure increases or decreases in equality metrics is important not only for maintaining pressure on organisations to address inequalities but also for tracking the effectiveness of measures introduced to offset them.

This trend for measuring gender inequality in quantitative terms was also rising to prominence in the UK in 2015. Seven months before the announcement of the 'Waking the Nation' programme in Dublin, Victoria Sadler published her first blog analysing the gender of playwrights at the National Theatre, the Old Vic, and the Donmar Warehouse in London.[66] Over a year later, she analysed the programmes of six major London theatres including the Young Vic, the

---

[65] https://the-lillys.org/the-count-2.
[66] https://web.archive.org/web/20200804161302/http://www.victoriasadler.com:80/female-play wrights-and-gender-inequality/.

Royal Court, and the Almeida alongside those already mentioned.[67] Her findings were poor everywhere except the Royal Court where Vicky Featherstone was championing female playwrights, with eight out of thirteen plays produced by the theatre in 2016 written by women and four of the six main stage plays written by women. Sadler's analysis created a stir among London theatre circles; however, unlike #WakingTheFeminists, her reports were part of a series of controversies rather than a watershed moment. At the same time as Sadler's first blog, the British Theatre Consortium, UK Theatre, and Society of London Theatre published a gender analysis of playwrights as part of their analysis of the British Theatre Repertoire in 2013. The report's findings, which revealed that only 31 per cent of new plays were written by women (2015), also provoked some surprise. The impact of these figures is no doubt due to the perception at the time that equality had been achieved: 'In 2008, when researching Writ Large we conducted interviews with some leading literary managers and artistic directors and asked if they had any policies to attract work by women; the consensus was that they didn't think there was a particular imbalance to correct' (British Theatre Consortium et al., 2015). The report also found that plays by women have tickets priced at 23 per cent lower, play in theatres that are 24 per cent smaller, and have a whopping 69 per cent fewer performances (British Theatre Consortium et al., 2015). A subsequent report on performances in 2014 confirmed that the previous year was not an anomaly. The 2014 report saw the number of solo-authored new plays by women remain at 31 per cent and while the capacity of theatres in which men's plays were produced rose, that of theatres where women's plays were produced fell (British Theatre Consortium et al., 2016). Men's plays also had a greater increase in the length of their runs and while average ticket prices for men's plays rose by 4 per cent, those for women fell by 1 per cent (British Theatre Consortium et al., 2016). Further research by Purple Seven found that in theatre in the UK, women 'account for 65 percent of ticket revenue, but only 39 percent of actors, 36 percent of directors and 28 percent of writers of plays' (2015). It also found that '[c]ritics award more 4 and 5 star ratings to plays with casts of their own gender [and male] Directors and Writers command bigger stages and higher ticket prices' (2015). Sphinx Theatre provided follow-up quantitative research in 2019 (Tuckett, 2019), which was published with three further reports containing qualitative research on women in UK theatre and recommendations for improving gender equality in the sector. This report found that in the UK in 2017–18, '31 percent of Artistic Directors of theatre NPOs [National Portfolio

---

Organisations] were female' but 'only 21 percent of NPO funding is controlled by female Artistic Directors' (Tuckett, 2019). Further reports, including Christine Hamilton's *Where Are the Women?*, analyse gender in Scottish theatre (Hamilton, 2016) and annual reports as part of the *Ou Sont Les Femmes?* Movement by the Société des Auteurs et Compositeurs Dramatiques in France[68] were also cited in *Gender Counts* as influences on its publication. The sheer volume of quantitative statistics reveals not only that #WakingTheFeminists' research was part of a significant trend of using statistical evidence to make equality arguments, but that Ireland had actually been lagging behind its nearest neighbours in publishing regular measurable data on women in theatre.

In the Foreword to *Gender Counts*, Lian Bell describes the report as 'the piece of the puzzle that was missing, the research that never existed' (Donohue et al., 2017: 5). Statistics had been central to the movement from the beginning, with many people and organisations counting their own histories and sharing the results on social media in the early weeks of the campaign. This continued throughout 2016, as new plays opening in Ireland shared the gender counts of their creative and production teams throughout their marketing. Six days after the 'Waking the Nation' launch, statistics on the low representation of women as playwrights at the national theatre were presented in a letter to *The Irish Times* by Brenda Donohue (2015). Donoghue found that between 1995 and 2014, 11 per cent of plays at the Abbey had been by women, and just 7 per cent of revived plays were by women (Donohue, 2015). A week later, statistics on the distribution of funding by gender were shared by Tríona Ní Dhuibhir on #WakingTheFeminists' website. Ní Dhuibhir revealed that while 65 per cent of the staff of Irish arts organisations are women and 59 per cent of CEOs were women, women only control 39 per cent of the funding: 'To put this more simply – for each €1 of public funding a woman CEO is charged with, her male counterpart is charged with €3.'[69] The most prominent response to these statistics was shock, even when the data were about an individual's own career. In a Facebook post from 29 October, later shared on Twitter, Charlotte McCurry shared her status as 'feeling shocked' with an account of her 'career math' that revealed that of the sixteen plays she had worked on, one was written by a woman and four were directed by women.[70] Among the most striking statements from a similar Facebook post by Donna Dent were: 'I have never been directed by a woman in theatre. I have never been in a new play by a woman.'[71]

---

[68] www.sacd.fr/fr/4%C3%A8me-%C3%A9dition-de-la-brochure-%C2%AB-o%C3%B9-sont-les-femmes-%C2%BB-pour-plus-d%C3%A9galit%C3%A9-dans-la-culture-la-sacd.

[69] www.wakingthefeminists.org/triona-ni-dhuibhir/.

[70] https://twitter.com/CharlieMcCurry/status/664100744438685696.

[71] https://twitter.com/lianbell/status/662970758885449729.

This was shared on Twitter by Lian Bell with a caption describing it as 'extraordinary'.[72] The shocking nature of these statistics was important as it provided a necessary jolt for a theatre community who had become complacent about gender equality.

On 5 November, Lisa Tierney-Keogh shared a poster describing the number of plays produced or presented by the Abbey Theatre since 2006.[73] The plays by men were listed in a tall column on the left, while plays by women were listed in a short column on the right. Tierney-Keogh and Charlie Veprek's findings showed that 12.6 per cent of plays at the Abbey were written by women.[74] A second graphic used the same layout to show the disparity between male and female directors at the Abbey, with women directing 19.6 per cent of plays since 2006. These posters are visually impactful with the disparity clear to the naked eye. This style of infographic design gives all the information in an apparently neutral way. The play titles, names of playwrights, stage, and year of first production are all presented in two simple lists, sorted by gender. D'Ignazio and Klein summarise the guidance advised for designers of data visualisations as: 'The more plain, the more neutral; the more neutral, the more objective; and the more objective, the more true' (D'Ignazio and Klein, 2020: 76). Tierney-Keogh and Veprek's poster uses this style to make this infographic appear incontestable and therefore highly convincing. These design choices also lend the image for sharing on social media where its simple message was circulated by Tierney-Keogh with the caption 'This is what inequality looks like'[75] and by Bell who wrote 'This. This is why.'[76] By transparently showing that women had been poorly represented in Abbey Theatre programmes over a period of ten years, Tierney-Keogh and Veprek presented their statistics as objective evidence that the exclusion of women's plays from these programmes was cultural and systemic, and not simply the result of there not being a play by a woman 'ready' or 'good enough' for the 2016 programme.

On 7 June 2017, #WakingTheFeminists' campaign reached its denouement with the launch of their research findings, *Gender Counts: An Analysis of Gender in Irish Theatre 2006–2015*. The report focussed on the top ten theatre organisations funded by The Arts Council/An Chomhairle Ealaíon in the Republic of Ireland, including two festivals, Dublin Theatre Festival and Dublin Fringe Festival; two producing houses, the Abbey Theatre and the Gate Theatre; one multi-disciplinary arts venue, Project Arts Centre; the

---

[72] https://twitter.com/lianbell/status/662970758885449729.

[73] https://twitter.com/lisatk/status/662319997574848512.

[74] www.wakingthefeminists.org/research/.

[75] https://twitter.com/lisatk/status/662319997574848512.

[76] https://twitter.com/lianbell/status/662354428503134210.

dedicated children's cultural centre, The Ark; and four theatre companies: Druid, Rough Magic Theatre Company, Barnstorm Theatre Company (focussed on theatre for young audiences), and Pan Pan Theatre. The data only considered companies in the Republic of Ireland, excluded dance and opera, and prioritised funding from the Arts Council to the exclusion of other funding sources. The report counted theatre productions that had more than five performances, ran for more than forty-five minutes, and were produced between 2006 and 2015; however, the diversity of these organisations resulted in some differences in how the numbers represent them. For instance, the theatre companies and producing houses listed earlier are fully responsible for their programmes, while the festivals and venues are reliant to some extent on the artistic producing decisions other companies are making. For The Ark, Project Arts Centre, and the Dublin Fringe Festival, theatre productions are only one part of their programme, so the numbers in *Gender Counts* only provide a partial representation of their output. Finally, because the theatre companies are led by artists who occupy key creative roles in most of their work, their figures for these roles tend to be skewed because of the over-representation of a single person in this role. For example, female representation for the role of Lighting Designer for Pan Pan is 100 per cent as this role is typically filled by Co-Artistic Director, Aedín Cosgrove, while female representation for the role of Director at the same company is 0 per cent as this role is typically filled by Co-Artistic Director, Gavin Quinn. There is also significant disparity in terms of the numbers of productions each organisation produces annually. While the festivals present large numbers of theatre productions each year (on average, thirty-nine for Dublin Fringe Festival (Donohue et al., 2017: 54)), a company such as Pan Pan Theatre produced on average three productions per year (Donohue et al., 2017: 57). Regardless of the differences between the organisations, the researchers were able to uncover a trend that linked gender inequality to levels of funding.

Despite the numerous women who offered testimonies of their experiences of sexism in the industry, and despite the obvious inequality of the 'Waking the Nation' programme, it was the statistics that offered the final, conclusive, and inarguable evidence that Irish theatre had an ongoing gender problem. For the ten years between 2006 and 2015, the report presented percentages for female representation across the roles of Authors (28 per cent), Directors (37 per cent), Cast (42 per cent), and the four major design disciplines, Set (40 per cent), Lighting (34 per cent), Costume (79 per cent), and Sound (9 per cent) for the ten organisations. In total, 1,155 productions were considered. Among the key findings, the researchers found 'an inverse relationship between levels of funding and female representation. In other words, the higher the funding an organisation receives, the lower the female presence' (Donohue et al., 2017: 7).

Gender Counts also presented some surprising results: '[T]he study does not find a link between female leadership in an organisation and female representation in the studied roles, which goes against what many of us assumed' (Donohue et al., 2017: 6). Like the women involved in The Women's Playwright's Forum and *There Are No Irish Women Playwrights!* who thought that having a woman in control of the Abbey Theatre would increase the number of plays by women in its programme, *Gender Counts*' research confirmed that this correlation does not always hold true.

At #WakingTheFeminists' final event, 'One Thing More', preliminary findings from the research for *Gender Counts* were presented by Tanya Dean, Brenda Donohue, and Ciara O'Dowd. The presentation included graphs visualising the representation of women in the ten organisations studied as overall figures and for the specific roles examined by the research. When the graph displaying the percentage of women in the Author category appeared, there was an audible gasp from the audience. Oonagh Murphy tweeted, 'The air just left the room in Abbey Auditorium as the figures for female artists revealed. Dramatic gasps at headline figures #wtfonething.'[77] Others tweeted, 'Gasps all round as The Gate, 2nd most funded company by arts council, has only 6 percent female authors and 8 percent directors #wtf #wtfonething.'[78] Kennedy and Hill's research on the *Seeing Data* project found that 'everyday engagements with data through visualisations evoke emotional responses that nuance the proposal that numbers alone are central to the logic of datafication. At the level of the everyday, *the feeling of numbers* is important' (Kennedy and Hill, 2018: 831). Six per cent *felt* like a surprisingly low representation of female playwrights at the Gate Theatre and it is this *feeling* that prompted the shocked reaction from the audience. While statistical data like this is invoked because of its objectivity, it is also affective in its influence.

Why did the data feel so shocking? Shock was a prominent response, not only to the research presented in *Gender Counts*, but even to the self-reflective 'career math' conducted by individuals. There seems to have been a disconnect evident throughout the controversy between the theatre community's perceived liberal, feminist identity, and its actual conservative, patriarchal reality. The reason this disconnect emerged is because, despite the experience of sexism on an individual level, for the most part, a majority male line-up looks familiar and, therefore, normal. Geena Davis, who founded the Geena Davis Institute to research unconscious gender biases in film and television, found that women only make up 17 per cent of crowds in G-rated animated movies (Tepper, 2013). That the same

---

[77] https://twitter.com/oonaghmurphy/status/798150978797191168.
[78] https://twitter.com/SiofraNicLiam/status/798150622734405633.

percentage of women recurred in other aspects of society including Fortune 500 boards, law partners, tenured professors, and even Congress led Davis to question whether this has become a norm (Davis, 2016). Davis found that 'in a group if there's 17 percent women, men think it's balanced. If there's 33 percent women, they think there's more women than men' (Wreyford, 2018: 46). When things are normal, they become invisible, and we stop noticing them. When the theatre sector does produce work that is liberal or feminist, it becomes salient because it is unusual, and that salience makes it more prominent in memory. So, when Fiach Mac Conghail was challenged on the male bias of his 2016 programme, he responded by listing all the women the theatre had supported over the years and the productions of plays by women it had recently programmed. It was not until he was presented with figures that revealed that these women made up such a small percentage of the total productions that he conceded the theatre's mistake. D'Ignazio and Klein describe the failure of those in powerful positions, like artistic directors, to identify instances of oppression as a 'privilege hazard' (D'Ignazio and Klein, 2020: 29). This is not to absolve Mac Conghail of responsibility for the gross disparity of the Abbey's programming during his tenure, but to illustrate the ease with which such disparity is normalised. I do not think that Mac Conghail believed that he was producing equal numbers of plays by women and men, but there does seem to be a sense in which he thought the theatre was being *fair enough* to women; that things weren't *that bad*. Without hard numbers, we rely on feelings to assess a situation. This is known as the affect heuristic, which occurs when 'people make judgements and decisions by consulting their emotions' (Kahneman, 2012: 139). Because Mac Conghail felt good about the plays by women he had produced, this feeling guided him to believe that the way the Abbey was serving women overall was good enough. In addition, because men have historically dominated public space and theatrical stages, the low numbers of plays by women felt right because it had been normalised.

#WakingTheFeminists' use of statistical data aligns it with similar research-informed initiatives in the theatre communities of Ireland's closest neighbours. However, it is only when the statistical data in *Gender Counts* is considered with the qualitative testimonies archived on #WakingTheFeminists' website that a full picture of the position of women in Irish theatre emerges. The quantitative data revealed that women were severely under-represented in many key artistic roles, particularly as playwrights and directors, but the qualitative data shows that this is not due to an absence of women, or their lack of engagement. The importance of the statistics, however, lay in their capacity to present the gender equality argument in numeric terms, which in turn provided a benchmark for the simple campaign message of 50:50 gender equality by 2020. However, with the plethora of quantitative data reporting similar kinds of figures in theatre in the USA, the UK, and

Ireland, there is a concern that these numbers become normalised. Porter writes that '[p]ublic statistics are able to describe social reality partly because they help to define it' (2020: 43), while D'Ignazio and Klein emphasise that '[p]roof can also unwittingly compound the harmful narratives [. . .] that are already circulating in the culture' (2020: 58). The more the figures of between twenty and thirty per cent women are circulated, the more normalised this ratio becomes, and the less shock is felt when these numbers are distributed. This is why #WakingTheFeminists' focus on systemic interventions, based on data, is so important. The introduction of clear targets, with deadlines, regular reporting, public accountability processes, and responsibility for gender equality resting with nominated staff members, all help to ensure that equality is accounted for by the system, and never normalised through faulty perception. This approach helped to ensure that this campaign would have a longer lasting impact than those of the past.

4 'Being Fair Takes Work': The Impact of #WakingTheFeminists

#WakingTheFeminists' impact on the Irish theatre industry has been significant, with the movement prompting policy changes in both theatre companies and funding agencies, thus penetrating the core of the sector's governing structures. Of the most significant developments, the publication by the Abbey Theatre of its 'Eight Guiding Principles for Gender Equality', followed by the publication of gender equality policies by nine Irish theatre organisations, represented a realisation of the recommendations of Iris Bohnet in *What Works* (2016). The appointment of one of the campaign's core members to the board of the Abbey Theatre in 2016, the call by Minister for the Arts, Heather Humphries, for all National Cultural Institutions to have gender equality policies in place by 2018, and the fact that equal opportunities, including gender equality, were made a condition of Arts Council funding in 2018 (Falvey, 2018) all attest to the campaign's infiltration of theatre policy from company to government level. That progress is beginning to show is evident from #WakingTheFeminists' second statistical report, *5 Years On: Gender in Irish Theatre – An Interim View*, which reveals an increase in the representation of women as writers and creators in all organisations (Murphy et al., 2020). #WakingTheFeminists' impact has also extended beyond representation by creating an environment in which abuses of power are now being publicly addressed. Most significantly, it has resulted in the establishment of a Code of Behaviour for handling allegations of abuse in the theatre workplace, an independent reporting facility for workers who have experienced bullying and/or harassment, as well as a number of initiatives addressing Irish theatre's racial and ethnic homogeneity.

Among the earliest signs of the campaign's success was the publication of the Abbey's 'Eight Guiding Principles for Gender Equality' on 30 August 2016.

The Principles contain a commitment to putting gender equality as a stated goal within the theatre's mission and memorandum and articles of association, to making gender equality a permanent board agenda item, to committing to gender equality in the play commissioning process, to achieve gender equality in all areas of the artistic programme over five-year periods, and to report on the progress of these initiatives in its annual reports (Abbey Theatre et al., 2018). These principles showed the national theatre in a leadership position on the issue of gender equality by providing a template from which other companies could derive their own policies. Following the establishment of the Gender Equality Policy Working Group in 2017, ten Irish theatre organisations launched their policies at an event at The Lir Academy in July 2018. Along with the Abbey Theatre were Cork Midsummer Festival, The Corn Exchange, Druid, Dublin Theatre Festival, The Everyman Theatre, Fishamble: The New Play Company, The Gate Theatre, The Lir Academy, and Rough Magic. While each organisation had a different approach, most adopted a commitment to ensuring gender equality over five-year periods; to publishing statistics annually; to making gender equality a permanent board agenda item; to appointing a member of staff to monitor gender equality; and to host gender equality or unconscious bias workshops for staff. Many theatre companies also advocated for ensuring gender balance when commissioning new work and introducing gender-blind casting where appropriate. Both Cork Midsummer Festival and Fishamble explicitly mention ensuring gender parity across projects of various scales, budgets, and prominence, while The Corn Exchange commits to a proactive approach to attracting more female sound designers by developing relationships, appointing the sound designer early in the process, and '[b]eing creative in finding other potential female sound designers through other artistic disciplines' (Abbey Theatre et al., 2018: 7). Through their commitment to the ongoing monitoring of gender equality, a clear timeline for parity, and the introduction of accountability for gender equality internally, to the board, and the public, these policies reflect the advice from behavioural research that data, deadlines, and knowing that someone is watching help to make goals achievable. They also reflect Bohnet's advice to adopt an 'unfreeze-change-refreeze' approach that involves reviewing current systems, changing them where necessary, and implementing new approaches that are subject to periodic reviews of their effectiveness (Bohnet, 2016: 58).

Of these ten organisations, only the training academy, The Lir, included a detailed section for 'Facilitating Non-Binary Students' in their policy (Abbey Theatre et al., 2018: 31). Each of the other policies have been written using binary terms, which, although perhaps revealing a generational difference in gender expression as well as reflecting the gendered composition of Irish theatre at that time, clearly exposes a blind spot that should be addressed sooner rather than later. Many organisations have also chosen to highlight gender-blind casting as a solution to the visibility of women on Irish stages. Although this does address the issue of employment inequality for actors and would improve the overall gender balance on individual productions, it brings both possibilities and limitations for the kinds of roles women can play. Furthermore, if gender-blind casting is not accompanied by a resolution to the problem of gendered authorship inequality, it could be seen as an attempt to paper over the absence of women's plays by making women's bodies more visible on stage.

The principles also included a commitment to deliver a workshop programme for employees on gender equality. While implicit bias workshops may be useful for educating people about how bias works, their effectiveness in actually addressing the issue is unproven. Bohnet summarises that '[a]t this point we have to conclude that diversity training either does not work or, at the very least, that we do not have enough evidence to know whether and under what conditions it does any good' (2016: 54). In fact, Bohnet cautions against their use in isolation of systemic change due to the tendency to view the workshop as the solution to the issue that results in moral licensing. Jennifer Eberhardt agrees with Bohnet, describing the effect of bias training in terms of the '"some of my best friends are black hall pass." If you've stored enough credits in the bank of equality, you're entitled to behave badly' (2020: 282). This human tendency to view an isolated action as evidence of changed behaviour means that bias training can lead people to believe that, by completing the training, they have addressed inequality and their confidence in being 'cured' of bias may manifest in displays of even more strongly biased behaviour than before.

#WakingTheFeminists set a target of 50:50 gender equality by 2020 for Irish theatre at their final event (Dawe, 2019–20). In some respects, this target was ambitious; however, the primary problem with the five-year target for parity is the ability for companies to postpone addressing the issue until a later date. The five-year programming term traverses not only multiple programmes but may traverse changes of staffing, producing climates, and even pandemics. What this means is that the decision to commit to gender equality must be made repeatedly, which increases the likelihood of failure. For companies like the Abbey, whose programme for 2019 for instance, included eleven main-stage productions, a commitment to gender equality in a single year seems both achievable and more manageable. While this may be more difficult to achieve for smaller companies, with only a handful of new productions a year, even reducing the timeline to every two years would make the aggregate target clearer. Advocating for smaller, interim goals, Bohnet explains that '[s]etting sub-goals has been found to have positive effects by increasing a sense of accomplishment, interest in a task, and persistence in achieving it' (2016: 279). She also observes that 'variety is more likely to emerge when people make multiple decisions simultaneously rather than sequentially' (Bohnet, 2016: 127). The benefits of grouping decision-making can already be seen from the short play initiatives introduced by organisations including Fishamble and the Abbey Theatre during the lockdowns imposed because of the Covid-19 pandemic in 2020. In each iteration of these productions, the gender of the playwrights was balanced, which proves the effectiveness of their strategies for their short play initiatives. This is particularly true for Fishamble whose Gender Equality Policy contains a very detailed strategy for short play initiatives, from preparation, throughout the process, to post-project review (Abbey Theatre et al., 2018: 20). While quotas are essential tools in the fight against gender equality, Bohnet points out that they are 'not behavioral interventions' (2016: 241). Quotas can be seen as ideals to aim for, rather than necessary baselines, and in the absence of policing can easily be ignored. Despite these issues, these policies represent an important step forward in ensuring that a commitment to gender equality is engrained within the structure of these organisations.

In November 2020, on the five-year anniversary of the first #WakingThe Feminists' Public Meeting, *5 Years On: Gender in Irish Theatre – An Interim View* was published. A follow-up to *Gender Counts*, the report focusses on how companies have fared with tackling gender inequality in the years since its publication through analysis of self-reported statistics for productions presented in 2017, 2018, and 2019. The publication of *5 Years On* revealed that for most, parity had not yet been reached, but that there was an overall increase in the percentage of work being created by women for all the organisations studied. The report emphasises that '[n]one of this has happened automatically, or by chance. It is the result of planning, accountability, and the consistent work of people counting, noting and making changes' (Murphy et al., 2020: 3). The most dramatic increase was seen at the Gate Theatre where, under the new artistic directorship of Selina Cartmell, the representation of women as directors increased from 8 to 68 per cent (Murphy et al., 2020: 3). The role of Sound Designer, which typically has the lowest representation of women also increased from 1 to 45 per cent at the Gate. The Abbey Theatre also saw positive changes with women more than doubling in the roles of Director, which increased from 20 to 46 per cent, and Creator, which rose from 17 to 35 per cent (Murphy et al., 2020: 5). Druid also saw an increase in women in the role of Creator from 13 to 30 per cent (Murphy et al., 2020: 7). The increase in Lighting Designers was also significant at Druid, where the representation of women rose from 3 to 22 per cent (Murphy et al., 2020: 7). While in *Gender Counts*, the statistics included just one non-binary individual, Dublin Theatre Festival reported that trans/non-binary artists made up 5 per cent of its Creators in 2019, and at Dublin Fringe Festival, non-binary artists comprised 2 per cent of their Ideas Generator[79] and Ideas Shaper[80] roles in 2019 (Murphy et al., 2020: 13). These increases prove that dramatic changes can be made quickly, and that the policy adjustments advocated by #WakingTheFeminists are working.

While #WakingTheFeminists adopted an inclusive approach to its organising and platforming, its strategic and research focus was on theatre in the Republic of Ireland. Therefore, a separate group, Waking the Feminists Northern Ireland, was formed in Belfast in June 2016 (Cronin, 2021: 6). Maggie Cronin notes that while there 'was an appetite for change from individuals working within the theatre sector in Northern Ireland', the response, 'to the findings of Waking the Feminists at company or funding agency level was more muted and lacked cohesion' (Cronin, 2021: 5). Cronin attributes this more subdued response to the particular socio-economic conditions in the North, including the bipartisan division of communities and the underfunding of, and political ambivalence towards, the arts (Cronin, 2021: 5). From the first meeting of Waking The Feminists NI, two distinct strands of activism emerged: the first focussed on sexual harassment and bullying; and the second involved the collection of data (Cronin, 2021: 6). The resulting research, *The Headcount: A Survey on the Gender Breakdown of Eight Arts Council of Northern Ireland Core-Funded Theatre Companies 2014–2019*, was published in 2021. It found that 64 per cent of directors in Northern Ireland's core-funded theatres were women.[81] This high level of representation can be attributed to the fact that five of the eight theatre companies surveyed are led by female artistic directors (Cronin, 2021: 9). The report found the representation of women in the following roles to be: Writers: 37 per cent; Cast: 47 per cent; Set Design: 41 per cent; Lighting Design: 22 per cent; Sound Design: 12 per cent; Costume Design: 79 per cent; Stage Manager: 81 per cent (Cronin, 2021: 9–12).[82] While these figures are higher than those presented in *Gender Counts*, the report concludes by noting that 'the Lyric, which is the highest funded company, has some of the lowest figures for female representation, particularly in the role of director and author' (Cronin, 2021: 48). This finding aligns with those of Tríona Ní Dhuibhir and Sphinx Theatre cited in Section 3, which agree that even when women comprise the majority of the workforce, it is men who still control the majority of the funding.

The ongoing production of quantitative data has been an important outcome of #WakingTheFeminists, as has the establishment of other affiliated groups

---

[79] Term used to encompass writers, choreographers, composers, devisors, etc.
[80] Term used to encompass directors, lead artists, etc.
[81] Percentages have been rounded for clarity.　　[82] Percentages have been rounded for clarity.

founded to address specific issues that arose during the campaign. At the first #WakingTheFeminists event, Tara Derrington raised a sign that said 'Where are the DISAPPEARED women of the arts? . . . At the school gates now.' In the days after the event, numerous women began to share their experiences as mothers and carers in the arts. Sinead McKenna summarised the consensus, saying 'For many it has been a choice between "career" and "carer."'[83] Among the many testimonies describing the difficulty in securing acting roles as mothers, Andrea Irvine revealed: '[T]he truth is that I had to give up on any idea of career or living wage since the day and hour I announced I was pregnant.'[84] Others touched on the particular issues of arranging childcare for the unpredictable and atypical hours of theatre work. Maree Kearns wrote: 'That structured childcare system just doesn't work for freelancers – for one thing you're not always working so why farm your child out somewhere they don't need to be and secondly you can't always afford it.'[85] Moyra D'Arcy added that the 'irregularity of the work' was also an issue. 'Finding childcare for random blocks of long hours and evening work is hard and stressful to organise.'[86] Led by Derrington, 250 female theatre practitioners united to form MAMs, Mothers Artists Makers, 'to highlight issues of domestic isolation, marginalisation, and the disproportionate impact of parenting on the salaries of mothers who work in theatre'.[87] The group found that '[a]fter having children, over half [the] members surveyed lost ALL their income from theatre. 95 percent of the rest suffered reduced incomes'.[88] The disproportionate impact of parenthood on women is widely documented, with women experiencing a 'child salary penalty' while men get a 'child salary premium' (Bohnet, 2016: 32). However, irregular hours, touring, and physical changes to the body can all amplify the salary penalties for mothers in theatre. At the Theatre Forum Conference in June 2017, Tara Derrington introduced MAM's 5 Family Friendly Practices Towards Gender Balanced Irish Theatre, which include recommendations to consider sympathetic scheduling, child-friendly work spaces, family friendly Front of House training, pop-up crèches, and to ask workers, '[i]s there anyone in your life whose care you are responsible for and is there any way we can assist you to facilitate this while you work for us?'[89] While the 5 Family Friendly Practices offer advice on how to support working

---

[83] https://twitter.com/WTFeminists/status/668767302242947072.
[84] https://twitter.com/WTFeminists/status/668767302242947072.
[85] https://twitter.com/WTFeminists/status/668767619370086400.
[86] https://twitter.com/WTFeminists/status/668767619370086400.
[87] www.wakingthefeminists.org/tara-derrington-one-thing-more-speech/.
[88] www.wakingthefeminists.org/tara-derrington-one-thing-more-speech/.
[89] https://mamsireland.wordpress.com/2017/07/13/5-family-friendly-practices-towards-gender-balanced-irish-theatre/.

parents, the underlying issues for mothers, particularly those who are actors, seeking employment remain.

While the formation of MAMs in part reflects the fact that issues of parenthood were not a prominent feature of #WakingTheFeminists, stories of sexism and harassment both in the workplace and on the street were an important part of the movement from the very beginning. At the International Women's Day meeting in 2016, Kate Ferris described the harassment female technicians are subjected to (#WakingTheFeminists, 2016b), Sonya Kelly gave humorous tips on how to avoid harassing people, while Una Mullally gave an impassioned speech driven by the violent assault of her housemate the previous weekend (#WakingTheFeminists, 2016a). While these testimonies began to lift the lid on women's experiences in misogynistic environments, it was not until the hashtag, #MeToo, went viral in 2017 that women began to publicly name their abusers. On 27 October 2017, seven Irish theatre organisations issued a joint statement in response to #MeToo allegations levelled against Harvey Weinstein in the US (first aired in *The New York Times* on 5 October) and Max Stafford Clark in the UK (reported in *The Guardian* on 20 October).[90] The same evening, Grace Dyas published a Tumblr post about her experience of sexism and harassment from the former Director of the Gate Theatre, Michael Colgan. Dyas' post was actually the fulfilment of a promise made at the first #WakingTheFeminists meeting, when Dyas said, 'I'm making a pledge here right now that I will hold people to account for misogyny, for bias, for inequality' (#WakingTheFeminists, 2015b). Deliberately placing her unwillingness to put up with Colgan's misogyny as a direct result of #WakingTheFeminists, Dyas wrote: 'It wasn't the same anymore. [...] #WTF might not have changed Michael, but it has changed me.'[91] Her post prompted a flurry of support online under the hashtag, #MeTooMC, and incited a number of other women to come forward with their stories. The level of public pressure created by #WakingTheFeminists had fostered a sense of urgency that any scandal relating to issues of gender inequality be dealt with swiftly, and in November, the Gate Theatre commissioned an independent review into the allegations. The findings of that review were published in a report by Gaye Cunningham on 1 March 2018, which found that Colgan 'has a case to answer in respect to dignity at work issues, abuse of power and inappropriate behaviours' (Cunningham, 2018). However, as Colgan had already retired and was no longer an employee of the organisation, there was little action the theatre could take against him.

---

[90] The statement was signed by Graham McLaren and Neil Murray from the Abbey Theatre, Garry Hynes from Druid Theatre, Kris Nelson from the Dublin Fringe Festival, Willie White from Dublin Theatre Festival, Selina Cartmell from the Gate Theatre, Cian O'Brien from Project Arts Centre, and Lynne Parker from Rough Magic Theatre Company.

[91] https://gracedyas.tumblr.com/page/3.

On 21 March 2018, just three weeks after this report was published, the Irish Theatre Institute presented a draft Code of Behaviour for the theatre sector that dealt with bullying, harassment, and abuse in the workplace.[92] This discussion document was subsequently ratified by the theatre sector at an event at Project Arts Centre on 31 October 2018. The Code was followed in 2021 by the publication of *Speak Up: A Call for Change*, which provided findings and recommendations based on a cross-artform survey of workplace experiences of bullying and harassment (Murphy et al., 2021). Workshops were organised around the country to support organisations in implementing the code along with a range of training programmes, covering topics including Tackling Bullying and Harassment, Addressing Unconscious Bias, Bystander Training, and Intimacy Coordination, as part of a Dignity at Work programme called Safe to Create.[93] Safe to Create also provides an online anonymous reporting tool for arts workers to report incidents of bullying and harassment.[94] The rapidity with which the Irish theatre community acted on the #MeToo allegations can be attributed to the new environment created by #WakingTheFeminists in which people are empowered to speak up about abuses of power. In a sector in which a predominantly freelance workforce does not have access to the same structural supports as salaried employees, the establishment of the Code of Behaviour and Safe to Create represents important steps towards providing safeguarding procedures for the unique conditions of theatre work.

Despite the fact that #WakingTheFeminists' focus was on the under-representation of women in Irish theatre, it also impacted the industry's awareness of the under-representation of various other minority groups. Amid the feverish energy of the first public meeting, some speakers offered forceful reminders to the group of their predominantly white, settled, and abled privilege. These women were the killjoys within the movement, occupying the role of the 'feminist killjoy who kills feminist joy' (Ahmed, 2017: 177). At the first public meeting, and on numerous occasions afterwards, Rosaleen McDonagh reminded #WakingTheFeminists not to repeat the mistakes of the patriarchal model by ensuring to include disabled women and women from marginalised backgrounds: 'As feminists in the arts, let's not replicate male behaviour by excluding certain categories of women.'[95] Mary Duffin's testimony, which relayed a litany of instances of racism she encountered in Irish theatre, was delivered with palpable emotion. She recalled wanting to direct plays with

---

[92] www.irishtheatreinstitute.ie/resources/speak-up-call-it-out/.
[93] www.safetocreate.ie/training-resources/training/.
[94] https://reportandsupport.safetocreate.ie/report.
[95] www.wakingthefeminists.org/rosaleen-mcdonagh/.

Black casts but was told 'it's been done' (#WakingTheFeminists, 2015a). Donna Anita Nikolaisen's speech was delivered by Leah Minto and emphasised her frustration as an actor being 'excluded from many roles in classic, period, and contemporary plays' due to her ethnicity.[96] Although the campaign's primary concern was with gender equality, in *Gender Counts*, Bell articulated that #WakingTheFeminists' 'hope and ambition was always that the organisational and psychological changes wrought in the wake of the campaign could also be taken advantage of by those who continue to be sidelined in our culture; because they are disabled, poor, transgender, a member of the Traveller community, or another minority' (Donohue et al., 2017: 6).

Reviewing the campaign in 2023, Ciara L. Murphy described 'the lack of diversity present on the stage' at #WakingTheFeminists' first public meeting as 'striking' (Murphy, 2023). While Emilie Pine lauded #WakingTheFeminists for drawing 'attention to multiple intersectional forms of inequality', she found that 'it was striking that the 600-strong crowd at the first WTF meeting was, as far as [she] could see, exclusively white' (Pine, 2020: 230). Despite these criticisms of the crowd gathered on stage and in the auditorium, I would argue that the movement has prompted the sector to take action to address its whiteness and its under-representation and misrepresentation of Travellers despite this not being a primary aim of the campaign. This is due in part to the important testimonies shared at the public meetings, and to the #BlackLivesMatter movement, which prompted marches in Dublin in 2020. That theatres are taking the issue seriously is evident from the Abbey Theatre's first production of a play by a Traveller, Rosaleen McDonagh's *Walls and Windows*, on the main stage in 2021, and from the introduction of a number of initiatives to develop work by artists of colour. Fishamble: The New Play Company, in partnership with the Irish Repertory Theatre in New York, commissioned four Black Irish artists and writers of colour to work with mentor, Dael Orlandersmith, to create new works as part of the Transatlantic Commissions programme.[97] Fishamble also provided paid workshops on writing for performance for artists who are Black, a person of colour, from an ethnic minority background, or from a migrant background, led by Gavin Kostick and poet and playwright, Felicia Olusanya (Felispeaks).[98] Smock Alley Theatre launched The Baptiste Programme, a paid script development programme for Black Irish theatre makers and writers of colour, facilitated by Dramaturg, Pamela McQueen.[99] Dublin Fringe Festival's Weft Studio is an initiative for Black artists and artists of colour in all

---

[96] www.wakingthefeminists.org/donna-anita-nikolaisen-wtf-international-womens-day/.
[97] www.fishamble.com/transatlantic-commissions-irishrep.html.
[98] www.fishamble.com/writingforperformance.html.
[99] https://smockalley.com/baptiste-programme/.

performance disciplines to create work, facilitated by playwright, Carys D Coburn.[100] While there have been many artists of colour and from minority ethnic backgrounds working in Irish theatre, and many Irish theatre companies who have been prominently concerned with making work by these artists, this wave of schemes designed to develop new work by artists from minority racial and ethnic backgrounds represents a significant shift in Irish theatre, which has undoubtedly been influenced by #WakingTheFeminists. The importance of these initiatives is that they have been instigated by established Irish theatre organisations who are actively and explicitly seeking people from minority racial and ethnic backgrounds to engage with them. However, as they are all aimed at the script development/workshop level, it is yet to be seen how well they translate into full productions. The introduction of these initiatives is not to say that Irish theatre does not have an issue with racism. When the Abbey Theatre produced Branden Jacobs-Jenkins' *An Octoroon*, their first production with a majority cast of colour, controversy arose when only the two white cast members were nominated at *The Irish Times* Irish Theatre Awards, which prompted the suspension of judging in 2023 (Carolan, 2023). Further criticism was levelled against the Abbey's production of *Ironbound* by Martyna Majok because of the theatre's consistent misrepresentation of Polish migrant voices, particularly those of Polish women (Lech, 2023). These controversies illustrate the urgency with which Irish theatre needs to take account of how it is treating people of colour and other immigrants and the necessity of diversifying its workforce.

The impact of #WakingTheFeminists spread beyond Ireland and beyond theatre, as international theatre organisations and other artforms nationally began to seriously reconsider gender inequality as an urgent issue. That #WakingTheFeminists was resonating with other artforms was evident from the start of the campaign with Bord Scannán na hÉireann/Irish Film Board releasing a statement recognising the major under-representation of women in Irish film on the morning of #WakingTheFeminists' first live event.[101] Inspired by #WakingTheFeminists, multiple groups working across the Irish culture industry have formed to address gender inequality in their artform. Sounding the Feminists (originally Composing the Feminists) was formed in 2016 in response to the under-representation of women in 'Composing the Island', a festival of music composed by Irish writers and co-produced by the National Concert Hall and RTÉ. Since its foundation, the collective has secured funding for a five-year initiative in partnership with the National Concert Hall to commission and programme female and female-identifying composers and musicians. In November 2023, they published *Uneven*

---

[100] www.fringefest.com/news/weft-studio-applications-now-open.
[101] www.scannain.com/irish/statement-from-the-irish-film-board-concerning-gender-equality-in-irish-film/.

Score – An Assessment of the Gender Balance for Publicly Funded Composer Opportunities on the Island of Ireland 2004–2019 (Lydon, 2023). Further initiatives addressing gender inequality in the music industry include the Why Not Her? Collective, who have begun producing annual reports on gender and racial disparity on Irish and UK radio stations, and FairPlé, an organisation set up in 2018 to achieve gender balance in Irish traditional and folk music. In 2018, Kenneth Keating and Ailbhe McDaid founded MEAS (Measuring Equality in the Arts Sector) to high-light representational inequalities in the arts sector, with particular focus on the literary arts.[102] A number of other groups including #WakeUpIrishPoetry, Comedy Safety Standards, Trans Writers Union, and Reawaken The Feminists united under the umbrella activist organisation Safe Arts of Ireland to 'help exhausted volunteer feminist activists in the Irish arts to help each other' (D'Arcy, 2022: 66). The organisation's mission is 'to address sexual harassment and inappropriate sexual conduct across all areas in the Irish arts world' (D'Arcy, 2022: 66). The emphasis on the production of data and on addressing bullying and harassment across these groups reflects the influence #WakingTheFeminists has had throughout the Irish arts.

#WakingTheFeminists' reach has extended across the island of Ireland, across communities, and across the arts sector. Its impact can be traced in the important policy changes in Irish theatre, in the adoption of data-driven campaigns in other artforms, and in a cultural shift in which people are now emboldened to hold organisations to account for inequalities and biases. While it might yet be too early to measure the long-term impact of the campaign, protocols are currently in place in many Irish theatre organisations to monitor those changes. With gender equality now a condition of Arts Council funding, the impetus to keep improving on existing numbers is strong. Caitríona McLaughlin said at #WakingTheFeminists' first Public Meeting that 'being fair takes work',[103] but what the structural changes implemented since the movement's formation have done is taken some of that work off the shoulders of individuals and embedded it within institutions. This should ensure the longevity of the campaign's legacy by making it impermeable to the whims and fancies of individual leaders.

Conclusion

At the final public event, historian Catriona Crowe reminded those gathered of the history of feminism in Ireland, which manifested in loud gestures like the digging of golf courses by Unionist women in the North, as well as the more

---

[102] https://measorg481844298.files.wordpress.com/2019/05/meascfp2019.pdf.

[103] www.wakingthefeminists.org/caitriona-mclaughlin-public-meeting-speech/.

reserved lobbying for changes in legislation. Addressing #WakingTheFeminists directly, Crowe remarked, 'In your approach and methodology, you have united the noisy and restrained strands of the previous waves of feminism. [. . .] And you have created a template for the rest of the feminist movement to follow: beautiful noise and super-smart evidence-based findings.'[104] The movement's combined use of social media and public meetings, of consciousness-raising testimonies and quantitative data, of celebrity star-power and bureaucratic lobbying, resulted in a high-profile campaign with a solid foundation. Revisiting The Women's Playwrights Forum, *There Are No Irish Women Playwrights!* and the 'abbeyonehundred' debacle makes it clear that #WakingTheFeminists benefitted from the advancements in research on unconscious biases and behavioural economics over the past three decades to create a campaign strategy focussed on changing systems, not minds. However, #WakingTheFeminists' success can be charted not only through policy and organisational changes in Irish theatre, but through a broader cultural change in the wider arts sector and beyond. These gains may be attributed in part to the timeliness of the movement's emergence during the favourable political, economic, and social conditions of late 2015. This auspicious moment, in which feminism's popularity was rising globally, Ireland's liberalism was dominating politics nationally, and impending changes in leadership at prominent Irish theatres were exciting the sector locally, created the conditions in which a movement for gender equality in Irish theatre could flourish.

While the movement has made an extraordinary impact on increasing the representation of women in many roles in Irish theatre, parity remains elusive. Two of the outstanding primary concerns facing women in theatre remain fair pay and affordable, flexible childcare. At the final public meeting, production manager and designer, Marie Tierney, commented: 'At current rates by the time this gender pay gap has closed, I will be 228 years old.'[105] Because of this, interventions will be necessary to improve parity in this area. While Fishamble, The Lir Academy, and Rough Magic showed good policies for monitoring pay parity in their Gender and Equality Policies, such protocols have not been implemented widely beyond the legal requirements for equitable remuneration. With regard to theatre, special attention needs to be paid not only to equal pay for specific roles, but for equal pay for comparative roles, for example, whether a lighting designer and costume designer are being compensated at the same rate, given equal contributions to a production. The introduction of gender into Theatre Forum's pay scales survey has not revealed information on the gender pay gap for specific roles, but it has found that 'most workers in Irish theatre are

[104] www.wakingthefeminists.org/catriona-crowe-one-thing-more-speech/.
[105] www.wakingthefeminists.org/marie-tierney-one-thing-more-speech/.

women, but that men stand a better chance of earning above €35,000 a year' (McCormack, 2016). Better transparency and reporting around pay scales will help to identify the nature and the extent of this issue. Wage discrepancies are compounded by the disproportionate care-burden placed on women, particularly on mothers. While the issue of childcare goes far beyond the theatre industry, and will require state-level solutions, the advice of MAMs offer interventions that theatres can implement now to better accommodate parents in the workplace. This, like many of the issues raised during the campaign, such as normalised gender inequality, pay disparity, and sexual harassment, is not specific to the theatre industry. But the ways in which these problems manifest in rehearsal rooms and theatres do raise issues that are unique to the performing arts sector. Because jobs for many theatre workers typically last for between six and eight weeks, hiring processes are less structured and more dependent on personal relationships than other sectors. Intimacy with co-workers is often required of actors, which makes boundaries between appropriate and inappropriate behaviour in rehearsal rooms more difficult to maintain. For an industry where work is unpredictable, hours are long, and travel is frequent, standardised childcare provision fails to meet the flexibility required for many workers. However, the improvements to opportunities for women, the introduction of reporting infrastructure for bullying and harassment, and the implementation of measures to increase Irish theatre's diversity show that, with some good-will, theatres can transform working conditions in a short space of time. In this instance, the short turnover of work in the industry makes it nimble, agile, and capable of making profound transformations with wide-reaching impact.

In *Look! It's a Woman Writer!*, Phyl Herbert remarked: 'It appears that there needs to be a constant Women Playwrights' Forum or a Waking the Feminists in existence to order for the gains made not to be lost, and for basic questions of equality and diversity to be asked of our theatre makers and funding bodies' (2021: 308). Some of the most significant interventions made by #WakingTheFeminists into changes in governance for Irish theatre organisations and policy for theatre funders should help to ensure that these basic questions are embedded in their organising structures. However, as Lia Mills commented, in the same volume, 'Every generation thinks it has found a solution but what actually happens is that the generation that follows then fails to see the problem. Before we know it, we're back where we started' (2021: 74). The quantitative data produced by #WakingTheFeminists are one of the important interventions into making sure that this very problem does not occur. The numbers help to counteract this problem by keeping the issue visible and quantifiable, and the implementation of Bohnet's recommendation to unfreeze, change, and refreeze should ensure the periodic testing and revision of gender equality initiatives as required. Because of the openness of #WakingTheFeminists' campaign, there was room for many dissenting voices. Among these were many critics of the introduction of quotas, which were frequently cited as an effective solution to gender inequality. Bohnet writes that when people think 'there is a "pipeline" problem, that there are too few qualified women for a given job, or that such mandates undermine the functioning of a team, you will expect quotas to decrease performance' (Bohnet, 2016: 236). Theatre, unlike many other industries, does not have a pipeline issue. Women comprise the majority of graduates on theatre programmes and make up the majority of the workforce in the sector as a whole. This means that quotas should work for theatre, because the supply of qualified women for the job is plentiful. However, as more working opportunities become available for women, attention needs to be given to who is getting these opportunities. #WakingTheFeminists' template for recording numeric data flattens out the variations of race, age, class, and ability within the category of 'women', and further testing for blind spots with regard to these variations may be required. While there are already a number of initiatives to address the poor representation of work by people of colour and from minority ethnic backgrounds in Irish theatre, different kinds of interventions may be required when addressing issues relating to class, ability, or age. Bohnet emphasises that '[w]e have not yet found the "one-size-fits-all" silver bullet' and that is why continuing to count, experiment with interventions, and test their effectiveness is so important (2016: 60).

From the earliest days of the campaign, an awareness of its significance, even as it was unfolding, was evident from the steps taken to preserve and archive its data. Lian Bell commented: 'We knew from the get go how important it was to ensure that #WakingTheFeminists was properly archived. We saw first-hand how easy it is for women's stories, women's voices, and women's achievements to be overlooked, and how quickly they fade' (Bell, 2021). Active documentation of the campaign's progression was evident throughout its evolution through the preservation of testimonies on its website, the video recordings of the live events, and the sharing of weekly Thursday updates on its social media channels to keep the wider community informed of offline activities. The value with which such documentation practice was held even formed one of the core points in 'Lian's List', which reminded companies and organisations to '[m]ake sure women are being properly credited for the work they do. Keep records. No one can count women unless archives are kept'.[106] This process guaranteed that this would not be another forgotten feminist furore, but an important point on the road to gender equality from which future campaigns could learn. The archiving

---

[106] www.wakingthefeminists.org/take-action/.

of #WakingTheFeminists' website as part of the National Library of Ireland's 'digital pilots project' consolidated the central significance of the movement as digital feminist activism. At the same time, the donation of some of the campaign's tangible material, like the banner from the first public meeting, to the National Museum of Ireland, preserves its physical history as one of value to the national story. Archiving the campaign material does not mean that the journey to gender equality is over or that there is no longer need for feminist agitation. It does, however, mark the extraordinary achievement of this movement, which grew from an impulsive Facebook post to a highly professional campaign that reached the heart of the Irish arts industry, reinvigorating its policies, and transforming its culture.

References

Abbey Theatre. (2015). *Waking the Nation – 2016 at the Abbey Theatre*. https://youtu.be/HL6_Bh2nQd0.

Abbey Theatre, Cork Midsummer Festival, The Corn Exchange, Druid, The Everyman Theatre, Dublin Theatre Festival, Fishamble: The New Play Company, The Gate Theatre, The Lir Academy, Rough Magic. (2018). *Gender Equality in Practice in Irish Theatre: The Policies*, www.dropbox.com/s/wujqugq48zndwse/Gender%20Equality%20in%20Action_The%20Policies.pdf?dl=0.

Ahmed, S. (2004). *The Cultural Politics of Emotion*. Edinburgh: Edinburgh University Press.

Ahmed, S. (2017). *Living a Feminist Life*. Durham: Duke University Press.

Armstrong, M. (2016). 'A Year on: What the Abbey Feminists Left in Their Wake', *Irish Independent*, 12 November, p. 13.

Banet-Weiser, S. and Portwood-Stacer, L. (2017). The Traffic in Feminism: An Introduction to the Commentary and Criticism on Popular Feminism. *Feminist Media Studies*, 17(5), 884–88.

Barnes, B. (2008). *Plays and Controversies: Abbey Theatre Diaries 2000–2005*. Dublin: Carysfort Press.

Bell, L. (2015). Just did a quick tot up of the Abbey's 2016 programme . . . Facebook post: *#WakingTheFeminists Collection*. National Library of Ireland.

Bell, L. (2021). *#WakingTheFeminists Archived – Lian Bell on Making History*, www.rte.ie/culture/2021/0122/1191427-wakingthefeminists-archive-national-library/.

Blake Knox, K. (2015a). *Abbey Hopes 1916 Programme Will Wake Nation*, www.independent.ie/entertainment/theatre-arts/abbey-hopes-1916-programme-will-wake-nation-34151255.html#:~:text=Abbey%20hopes%201916%20programme%20will%20Wake%20nation.

Blake Knox, K. (2015b). Abbey Sets Stage for Its Centenary, *Irish Independent*, 31 October, p. 13.

Bohnet, I. (2016). *What Works: Gender Equality by Design*. Cambridge, MA: The Belknap Press of Harvard University Press.

Boland, E. (1989). *A Kind of Scar: The Woman Poet in a National Tradition*. Dublin: Attic.

British Theatre Consortium, SOLT/UKTheatre, and BON Culture. (2016). *British Theatre Repertoire 2014*. https://static1.squarespace.com/static/

513c543ce4b0abff73bc0a82/t/57347c792b8dde48ff9c18e1/1463057537574/
British+Theatre+Repertoire+2014.pdf.

British Theatre Consortium, UK Theatre, and the Society of London Theatre. (2015). *British Theatre Repertoire 2013*. https://static1.squarespace.com/static/513c543ce4b0abff73bc0a82/t/55551653e4b0c8565f6fb1ff/143163963570 6/British+Theatre+Repertoire+2013.pdf.

Burns, J. (2015). Abbey's Mac Conghail and McKeon Stage Twitter Battle, *Sunday Times*, 1 November, p. 22.

Carolan, M. (2023). Irish Theatre Awards Judging for 2023 Paused while Review of Process Takes Place, www.irishtimes.com/culture/stage/2023/02/20/irish-theatre-awards-judging-for-2023-paused-while-review-of-process-takes-place/#:~:text=A%20statement%20from%20The%20Irish,judging%20process%20has%20been%20paused.

Castells, M. (2015). *Networks of Outrage and Hope*: *Social Movements in the Internet Age*. Cambridge: Polity Press.

Chamberlain, P. (2017). *The Feminist Fourth Wave*: *Affective Temporality*. Cham: Palgrave Macmillan.

Clare, D., McDonagh, F. and Nakase, J. (2021). Introduction. In Clare, D., McDonagh, F. and Nakase, J., eds., *The Golden Thread*: *Irish Women Playwrights Volume 1 (1716–1992)*. Liverpool: Liverpool University Press, pp. 1–14.

Clark-Parsons, R. (2022). *Networked Feminism: How Digital Media Makers Transformed Gender Justice Movements*. Berkeley, CA: University of California Press.

Coen, R. (2015). *Irish Consumers on Social Media – The Stats*, www.emarkable.ie/2015/08/irish-consumers-on-social-media-the-stats/?cn-reloaded=1.

Connor, C. (ed.). (2009). *Women Playwrights at the Abbey 1904–2004*. Cellbridge: Hecuba.

'Cringe' (2006). *Oxford English Dictionary*. Oxford: Oxford University Press.

Cronin, M. (2021). *The Headcount*: *A Survey on the Gender Breakdown of Eight Arts Council of Northern Ireland Core-Funded Theatre Companies 2014–2019*: Waking The Feminists NI. https://culturalpolicyireland.org/2021/11/29/waking-the-feminists-the-headcount-report/.

Cunningham, G. (2018). *Gate Theatre*: *Confidential Independent Review*. https://gatetheatre.ie/wp-content/uploads/2018/03/Independent-Review-Report-into-Gate-Theatre-by-Gaye-Cunningham-1.pdf

D'Arcy, K. (2022). #WakeUpIrishPoetry: Austerity and Activism in Contemporary Irish Poetry – A Personal Reflection. In Flynn, D. E. and Murphy, C. L., eds., *Austerity and Irish Women's Writing and Culture, 1980–2020*. London: Routledge, 54–75.

D'Ignazio, C. and Klein, L. F. (2020). *Data Feminism*. Cambridge, MA: The MIT Press.

Davis, G. (2016). Addressing Unconscious Bias. *McKinsey Quarterly* (February), www.mckinsey.com/~/media/McKinsey/Business%20Functions/ Organization/Our%20Insights/Addressing%20unconscious%20bias/Addressing %20unconscious%20bias.pdf.

Dawe, O. (2019–20). Perspectives on Practice: Converting Advocacy to Action: #WakingTheFeminists Legacy. *Irish Journal of Arts Management and Cultural Policy*, 7, 28–42.

Deegan, G. and Mackin, L. (2015). Abbey Had Good Year in 2014 with 1 m Profit, *The Irish Times*, 13 November, p. 5.

Delaney, J. (2015). 'Letters: Women and the Abbey Theatre', *The Irish Times*, 5 November, p. 17.

Donohue, B. (2015). *Women and the Abbey Theatre*, www.irishtimes.com/ opinion/letters/women-and-the-abbey-theatre-1.2415780.

Donohue, B., O'Dowd, C., Dean, T., et al. (2017). *Gender Counts: An Analysis of Gender in Irish Theatre 2006–2015*, www.dropbox.com/s/enznau2g2eou saa/WTF_Gender_Counts_2017_2ndEd_WEB.pdf?dl=0.

Eberhardt, J. L. (2020). *Biased: Uncovering the Hidden Prejudice That Shapes What We See, Think, and Do*. London: Penguin Books.

Falvey, D. (2018). *Yes We Did: Irish Theatre's Gender-Equality Revolution*, www.irishtimes.com/culture/stage/yes-we-did-irish-theatre-s-gender-equal ity-revolution-1.3563784.

Fotopoulou, A. (2016). *Feminist Activism and Digital Networks: Between Empowerment and Vulnerability*. London: Palgrave Macmillan.

Gerbaudo, P. (2012). *Tweets and the Streets: Social Media and Contemporary Activism*. London: Pluto Press.

Glassberg Sands, E. (2009). *Opening the Curtain on Playwright Gender: An Integrated Economic Analysis of Discrimination in American Theater*. Unpublished Undergraduate Thesis. Princeton University. https://graphics8 .nytimes.com/packages/pdf/theater/Openingthecurtain.pdf.

Hamilton, C. (2016). *Where Are the Women? Analysis of Creative Roles by Gender in Scottish Theatre 2014/15*, https://web.archive.org/web/20161025 223804/https://www.christinehamiltonconsulting.com/wp-content/uploads/ 2016/03/Where-are-the-women_-8-March-2016-1.pdf.

Haraway, D. (1988). Situated Knowledges: The Science Question in Feminism and the Privilege of Partial Perspective. *Feminist Studies*, 14(3), 575–99.

Haughton, M. (2018). 'Them the Breaks': #WakingTheFeminists and Staging the Easter/Estrogen Rising. *Contemporary Theatre Review*, 28(3), 345–54.

Hayes, K. (2015). 'Playing Unfair', *Sunday Times*, 22 November, p. 8.

Herbert, P. (2021). The Fruit of a Life. In Ní Dhuibhne, É., ed., *Look! It's a Woman Writer! Irish Literary Feminisms, 1970–2020*. Dublin: Arlen House, 295–310.

Jordan, J. and Stump, R. (2015). *The Count 1.0: The Lillys and the Dramatists Guild*, https://static1.squarespace.com/static/5bcf6521ebfc7f9408a5d08f/t/5bd008359140b7dc42c08f0c/1540360248319/The+Count+0–1.pdf.

Kahneman, D. (2012). *Thinking, Fast and Slow*. London: Penguin.

Kalim, S. (2023). Sticky Hashtags: The Role of Emotions and Affect in Hashtag Activism. In McDuffie, K. and Ames, M., eds., *Hashtag Activism Interrogated and Embodied: Case Studies on Social Justice Movements*. Denver, CO: University Press of Colorado, 38–51.

Kay, J. B. (2019). Introduction: Anger, Media, and Feminism: The Gender Politics of Mediated Rage. *Feminist Media Studies*, 19(4), 591–615.

Kay, J. B. and Banet-Weiser, S. (2019). Feminist Anger and Feminist Respair. *Feminist Media Studies*, 19(4), 603–609.

Kennedy, H. and Hill, R. L. (2018). The Feeling of Numbers: Emotions in Everyday Engagements with Data and Their Visualisation. *Sociology*, 52(4), 830–48.

Kiberd, D. (1995). *Inventing Ireland: The Literature of the Modern Nation*. London: Vintage.

Kilroy, T., Dawe, G., Henderson, L., et al. (1995). Don't Worry, Be Abbey. *Fortnight*, (336), 32–35.

Knops, L. (2023). Towards an Affective Turn in Theories of Representation: The Case of Indignation. *Representation*, 59(2), 271–88.

Lech, K. (2023). *Polish People Deserve Better from Irish Theatre ...*, https://thetheatretimes.com/polish-people-deserve-better-from-irish-theatre/.

Lorde, A. (1981). The Uses of Anger. *Women's Studies Quarterly*, 9(3), 7–10. *CUNY Academic Works*.

Lydon, M. (2023). *Uneven Score: An Assessment of the Gender Balance for Publicly Funded Composer Opportunities on the Island of Ireland 2004–2019: Sounding the Feminists and Contemporary Music Centre*, www.cmc.ie/sites/default/files/inline-media/cmc_uneven_score_report_v7.pdf.

Maples, H. (2011). *Culture War: Conflict, Commemoration and the Contemporary Abbey Theatre: Reimagining Ireland*. Bern: Peter Lang.

McCormack, C. (2016). *Waking the Feminists: 'Gender Equality in Irish Theatre Achievable in Five Years'*, www.thestage.co.uk/news/waking-the-feminists-gender-equality-in-irish-theatre-achievable-in-five-years.

Meany, H. (2018). *Waking the Feminists*: *The Campaign that Revolutionised Irish Theatre*, www.theguardian.com/stage/2018/jan/05/feminist-irish-theatre-selina-cartmell-gate-theatre.

Mills, L. (2021). The World Split Open. In Ní Dhuibhne, É., ed., *Look! It's a Woman Writer! Irish Literary Feminisms, 1970–2020*. Dublin: Arlen House, 59–78.

Morash, C. (2002). *A History of Irish Theatre, 1601–2000*. Cambridge: Cambridge University Press.

Moynihan, M. (2018). *How Waking the Feminists Set an Equality Agenda for Irish Theatre*, www.rte.ie/brainstorm/2018/1122/1012586-how-waking-the-feminists-set-an-equality-agenda-for-irish-theatre/.

Mullally, U. (2015). *Abbey Theatre Celebrates 1916 Centenary with Only One Woman Playwright*, www.irishtimes.com/opinion/una-mullally-abbey-theatre-celebrates-1916-centenary-with-only-one-woman-playwright-1.2413277.

Mullally, U. (2016). 'Waking the Feminists: Rebellion as Citizenship', *The Irish Times*, 29 October, p. 19.

Mulrooney, D. (2004). *Sin Bin*: *Play Boys – But Few Play Women*, Sunday Business Post, 18 January.

Munro, E. (2013). Feminism: A Fourth Wave? *Political Insight*, 4(2), 22–25.

Murphy, J. (2015). *Letters*: *Women and the Abbey Theatre*, www.irishtimes.com/opinion/letters/women-and-the-abbey-theatre-1.2415780.

Murphy, C. L. (2023). *Performing Social Change on the Island of Ireland*: *From Republic to Pandemic*. London: Routledge. www.taylorfrancis.com/books/9781003211679.

Murphy, C. L., Donohue, B., Ó Duibhir, C., Campbell, P. and Dawe, O. (2021). *Speak Up*: *A Call for Change. Towards Creating a Safe and Respectful Working Environment for the Arts*: Irish Theatre Institute, www.irishtheatreinstitute.ie/wp-content/uploads/2021/10/ITI-Speak-Up-A-Call-for-Change-Report-Oct2021_Final_WEB.pdf.

Murphy, C. L., O'Dowd, C., Donohue, B. and Durcan, S. (2020). *5 Years On*: *Gender in Irish Theatre – An Interim View*: #WakingTheFeminists, www.wakingthefeminists.org/wp-content/uploads/2020/11/5-Years-On_-Gender-in-Irish-Theatre-FINAL.pdf.

Myers, K. (2015). 'So, Where Are All These Brilliant Female Playwrights?' *Sunday Times*, 15 November, p. 31.

Nakase, J. (2017). *Women in Irish Theatre*: *No More Waiting in the Wings*, www.irishtimes.com/culture/books/women-in-irish-theatre-no-more-waiting-in-the-wings-1.3126448.

Ní Dhuibhne, É. (2021). Introduction. In Ní Dhuibhne, É., ed., *Look! It's a Woman Writer! Irish Literary Feminisms, 1970–2020*. Dublin: Arlen House, 13–34.

O'Toole, E. (2017). Waking the Feminists: Re-imagining the Space of the National Theatre in the Era of the Celtic Phoenix. *Lit: Literature Interpretation Theory*, 28(2), 134–52.

Orgad, S. and Gill, R. (2019). Safety Valves for Mediated Female Rage in the #Metoo Era. *Feminist Media Studies*, 19(4), 596–603.

Papacharissi, Z. (2015). *Affective Publics: Sentiment, Technology, and Politics*. New York: Oxford University Press.

Pine, E. (2020). *The Memory Marketplace: Witnessing Pain in Contemporary Irish and International Theatre*. Bloomington, IN: Indiana University Press.

Porter, T. M. (2020). *Trust in Numbers: The Pursuit of Objectivity in Science and Public Life*, new ed. Princeton, NJ: Princeton University Press.

Purple Seven. (2015). *Gender in Theatre*.

Quigley, C. (2018). #WakingTheFeminists. In Jordan, E. and Weitz, E., eds., *The Palgrave Handbook of Contemporary Irish Theatre and Performance*. London: Palgrave Macmillan, 85–91.

Rippon, G. (2019). *The Gendered Brain: The New Neuroscience that Shatters the Myth of the Female Brain*. London: Bodley Head, www.amazon.co.uk/dp/B07HMDQGC1?tag=prhmarketing2552-21.

'Shame' (2006). *Oxford English Dictionary*. Oxford: Oxford University Press.

Sihra, M. (2018). *Marina Carr: Pastures of the Unknown*. Cham, Switzerland: Palgrave Macmillan.

Smith, G. (2003). 'Abbey Gets in Gear for Centenary', *The Irish Times*, 22 November, p. 57.

Tepper, A. (2013). *Geena Davis Wants More Girls in Toons*, https://variety.com/2013/biz/news/geena-davis-gender-equality-in-media-1200502314/.

Tuckett, J. (2019). *What Share of the Cake*: Sphinx, https://sphinxtheatre.co.uk/wp-content/uploads/2020/02/What-Share-of-The-Cake...pdf.

#WakingTheFeminists (2015a). #WakingtheFeminists Public Meeting Part 1. www.youtube.com/watch?v=7uVwuEuBmn4.

#WakingTheFeminists (2015b). #WakingTheFeminists Public Meeting Part 2. www.youtube.com/watch?v=CpNJTvfOWDY.

#WakingTheFeminists (2016a). Part 2: #WakingTheFeminists at Liberty Hall 8 March 2016. www.youtube.com/watch?v=65E9KHvQGoA.

#WakingTheFeminists (2016b). Part 3: #WakingTheFeminists at Liberty Hall 8 March 2016. www.youtube.com/watch?v=b1R4GLGAf9Q.

Weckler, A. (2015). *Irish Mobile Phone Usage Highest in the Western World, Global Stats Reveal*, www.independent.ie/business/technology/irish-mobile-phone-usage-highest-in-the-western-world-global-stats-reveal/31480385.html.

White, V. (1993). Cathleen Ni Houlihan Is Not a Playwright. *Theatre Ireland*, (30), 26–29.

Williams, C., Hayes, K., Quill, S. and Dowling, C. (2001). People in Glasshouse: An Anecdotal History of an Independent Theatre Company. In Bolger, D., ed., *Druids, Dudes, and Beauty Queens: The Changing Face of Irish Theatre*. Dublin: New Island, 132–47.

Wreyford, N. (2018). *Gender Inequality in Screenwriting Work*. Cham: Springer Nature.

Yeats, W. B. (1991). Cathleen Ni Houlihan, in Harrington, J. P., ed., *Modern Irish Drama*, Norton Critical Edition. New York: Norton, 3–11.

Cambridge Elements ⹅

Women Theatre Makers

Elaine Aston
Lancaster University

Elaine Aston is internationally acclaimed for her feminism and theatre research. Her monographs include *Caryl Churchill* (1997); *Feminism and Theatre* (1995); *Feminist Theatre Practice* (1999); *Feminist Views on the English Stage* (2003); and *Restaging Feminisms* (2020). She has served as Senior Editor of Theatre Research International (2010–12) and President of the International Federation for Theatre Research (2019–23).

Melissa Sihra
Trinity College Dublin

Melissa Sihra is Associate Professor in Drama and Theatre Studies at Trinity College Dublin. She is author of *Marina Carr: Pastures of the Unknown* (2018) and editor of *Women in Irish Drama: A Century of Authorship and Representation* (2007). She was President of the Irish Society for Theatre Research (2011–15) and is currently researching a feminist historiography of the Irish playwright and co-founder of the Abbey Theatre, Lady Augusta Gregory.

Advisory Board

About the Series

This innovative, inclusive series showcases women-identifying theatre makers from around the world. Expansive in chronological and geographical scope, the series encompasses practitioners from the late nineteenth century onwards and addresses a global, comprehensive range of creatives – from playwrights and performers to directors and designers.

Cambridge Elements

Women Theatre Makers

Elements in the Series

A full series listing is available at: www.cambridge.org/EWTM

Printed in the United States
by Baker & Taylor Publisher Services